The
Poetry
of
Love

MEN and WOMEN: The Poetry of Love

Selected and edited, with notes by

Louis Untermeyer

and illustrated by

Robert J. Lee

American Heritage Press
A Subsidiary of McGraw-Hill

ACKNOWLEDGMENTS

ANTIOCH REVIEW for "Crystal Anniversary" by Philip Appleman. The poem first appeared in *Antioch Review*, Volume XXVI, Number 2, and was later incorporated in Philip Appleman's *Summer Love and Surf* published by Vanderbilt University Press in 1968.

NANCY CARDOZO for "Day Dream" from the sequence entitled "Letter from a Far Country."

JONATHAN CAPE LTD. on behalf of the Executors of the James Joyce Estate for "O sweetheart, hear you" and "O, it was out by Donnycarny" from *Chamber Music* by James Joyce.

J. M. DENT & SONS LTD. for "That Reminds Me" from *The Face Is Familiar* by Ogden Nash.

DODD, MEAD & CO. for "The Hill" by Rupert Brooke, from *The Collected Poems of Rupert Brooke*. Copyright © 1915 by Dodd, Mead & Co.; copyright renewed 1943 by Edward Marsh.

DOUBLEDAY & CO., INC. for "I Knew a Woman" by Theodore Roethke, Copyright © 1954 by Theodore Roethke, from *The Collected Poems of Theodore Roethke*, reprinted by permission of Doubleday & Co., Inc.

FABER AND FABER LTD. for "Stop All the Clocks" from *Collected Shorter Poems 1927–1957* by W. H. Auden; for "A Virginal" from *Personae* by Ezra Pound; for "I Knew a Woman" from *The Collected Poems of Theodore Roethke*.

HAMISH HAMILTON LTD. for "Imperial Adam" from *Poems*, Copyright © by A. D. Hope and Hamish Hamilton Ltd., London.

HARCOURT, BRACE & WORLD, INC. for "somewhere i have never travelled" from *Poems 1923–54* by E. E. Cummings. Copyright © 1931, 1959 by E. E. Cummings; for "Folk Song" from *Long Feud* by Louis Untermeyer, Copyright © 1914 by Harcourt, Brace & World, Inc., Copyright © 1942 by Louis Untermeyer; for "To a Weeping Willow" from *Long Feud* by Louis Untermeyer, Copyright © 1917, 1945 by Louis Untermeyer; for "The Dark Chamber" and "Equals" from *Long Feud* by Louis Untermeyer. Copyright © 1928 by Harcourt, Brace & World, Inc., Copyright © 1956 by Louis Untermeyer. The preceding poems reprinted by permission of Harcourt, Brace & World, Inc.

HARPER & ROW for "Mementos, 1" from *After Experience* by W. D. Snodgrass. Copyright © 1960 by W. D. Snodgrass and reprinted by permission of Harper & Row, publishers.

HOLT, RINEHART AND WINSTON, INC. for "The Silken Tent" from *Complete Poems of Robert Frost*. Copyright © 1942 by Robert Frost.

IV

"Stop All the Clocks" from *Collected Shorter Poems 1927–1957* by W. H. Auden.

RUTGERS UNIVERSITY PRESS for "All the Tree's Hands" from *Emblems of Passage* by Jeannette Nichols.

SIDGWICK & JACKSON LTD. for "The Hill" from *The Collected Poems of Rupert Brooke*.

SIMON & SCHUSTER, INC. for "Rondeau" from *Labyrinth of Love* by Louis Untermeyer. Copyright © 1965 by Louis Untermeyer.

THE SOCIETY OF AUTHORS for "When I was one-and-twenty," "White in the Moon," "Is my team ploughing," "O when I was in love with you," "Bredon Hill," "The True Lover," from A *Shropshire Lad* by A. E. Housman, reprinted by permission of The Society of Authors as the literary representative of the estate of A. E. Housman, and Jonathan Cape Ltd., publishers of A. E. Housman's *Collected Poems*.

JON STALLWORTHY for "Elegy for a Mis-spent Youth," originally published in the London *Times Literary Supplement*. Copyright by Jon Stallworthy.

THE VIKING PRESS, INC. for "Travel" from *Selected Poems 1956–1968* by Leonard Cohen; for "Imperial Adam" from *Collected Poems 1930–1965* by A. D. Hope; for "O sweetheart, hear you" and "O, it was out by Donnycarny" from *Collected Poems* by James Joyce, Copyright © 1918 by B. W. Huebsch, Inc., and renewed 1946 by Nora Joyce; for "Love on the Farm" by D. H. Lawrence from *The Complete Poems of D. H. Lawrence, Volume 1* edited by Vivian de Sola Pinto and F. Warren Roberts. Copyright © 1920 by B. W. Huebsch, Inc., renewed 1948 by Frieda Lawrence. The preceding poems reprinted by permission of The Viking Press.

A. P. WATT & SON for "When You Are Old" from *The Collected Poems of W. B. Yeats*, reprinted by permission of Mr. M. B. Yeats, owner of the copyright, and Macmillan Company, London, and Macmillan Company, Canada.

ANNA WICKHAM for the poems originally published in *The Contemplative Quarry* and *The Man with a Hammer*, reprinted by permission.

THE WORLD PUBLISHING COMPANY for "True Love" from *It's Hard to be Hip Over Thirty & Other Tragedies of Married Life* by Judith Viorst. Copyright © 1968 by Judith Viorst. An NAL book.

A FOREWORD

No emotion has elicited a wider expression and a greater response than that of love between men and women. Its literature is inexhaustible; that nothing new can be said about love has never stopped a poet from saying it again. Love is the world's favorite theme, and variations on it have been composed ever since man discovered the use of words.

Love's pain and ecstasy are ageless. The plaintive cry of a girl comes to us in an appeal found on a piece of papyrus three thousand years old.

> I trouble myself no longer over
> My hair dressing. Yet if you still
> Care, I will put on my curls,
> So I may be ready at any time.

Time cannot lessen the longing, the reaching out for affection. Every person has felt it, and every poet has extolled it in his own idiom. Browning put it in two lines:

> O lyric love, half angel and half bird,
> And all a wonder and a wild desire!

Other poets expatiated on love's ever-varied disclosures. As long ago as the first century B.C., Virgil declared, "Love conquers all things." Almost a thousand years before Virgil, a Hebrew rhapsodist (some say Solomon) composed the Song of Songs which told that "many waters cannot quench love, neither can the floods drown it." Shakespeare said it in one of his sonnets:

> Love's not Time's fool, though rosy lips and cheeks
> Within his bending sickle's compass come;
> Love alters not with his brief hours and weeks,
> But bears it out even to the edge of doom.

In A Midsummer Night's Dream Shakespeare let the unhappy Helena explain Cupid's traditional blindness:

> Love looks not with the eye but with the mind,
> And therefore is wing'd Cupid painted blind.

Donne believed not only in love's constancy but in its continuity:

> All other things to their destruction draw;
>   Only our love hath no decay.
> This, no tomorrow hath, nor yesterday,
> Running, it never runs from us away,
> But truly keeps his first, last, everlasting day.

Swift both acknowledged and resented the tender tyranny as well as the delusions of love when he wrote:

> In all I wish, how happy should I be,
> Thou grand Deluder, were it not for thee!
> So weak art thou that fools thy power despise,
> And yet so strong thou triumph'st o'er the wise.

Byron maintained that the two sexes were affected by two different responses:

> Man's love is of man's life a thing apart;
> 'Tis woman's whole existence.

Emily Dickinson affirmed this in a terse sentence:

> That love is all there is
> Is all we know of love.

Robert Bridges called on every lover with an appeal like a commandment:

> Live thou thy life beneath the making sun
> Till Beauty, Truth, and Love in thee are one.

It was with simple lyrics that the poetry of love began. As the singers became more sophisticated their songs grew more artful. The love-making of the Elizabethan poets was undoubtedly real, but all too many of their countless love-lyrics were not made of real passion but pastiche. The Fair Ones they extolled were indistinguishable from each other. All seem to have had bosoms of the whitest snow, foreheads of pure ivory, eyes that were stars and sapphires, cheeks of lilies and roses—Thomas Campion went so far as to say of his mistress: "There is a garden in her face!" If the poets are to be taken literally, the ladies of the period were persons without personality, figures as abstract as figures of speech. The high-born object of adoration was always supremely beautiful and superbly unattainable, while the ever-present shepherds and shepherdesses were as conventionally coy and unconvincing as their Dresden china counterparts.

Following the fashion, poets gave fictitious names to their inamorata. In daily life their real names were Susan and Barbara and Marjorie—

their intimates probably called them Sukie and Babs and Mardi—but such names were not fancy enough. As a result we have an almost endless parade of Chloes, Corinnas, Campaspes, Antheas, Amaranthas, Electras, Perillas, and Dianemes—names that were chosen partly as a discreet disguise but chiefly for their musical syllables.

Consequently even the least notable of sixteenth and seventeenth century love lyrics have a graceful melodiousness, a euphony enhanced by Herrick and such Cavalier poets as Waller, Suckling, Lovelace, and Marvell. A more intellectual intensity was sounded by Donne, while the Age of Reason, ushered in by Dryden and Pope, made even the irrationality of love sound reasonable. Blake restored pure vision to the poetry of love; Byron emphasized its romanticism, Shelly its exuberance, and Keats its ecstasy.

The poets reflect love's unpredictable and often contrary moods, its eager anticipation and rapt consummation as well as unrequited ardor. The emotions expressed range from fear to fulfillment, from the delight of complete possession to the anguish of loss. They include teasing comedy as well as consummation, for lovers' protestations are not without exaggerated vows. Mostly, however, they are cries from the heart: passionate appeals, lyric confessions, transports of joy. Their manifestations include the happiness of the moment and sad remembrance of the past, the sprightliness of Suckling's "Ballad upon a Wedding" as well as Yeats' contemplative "When You are Old." The poets speak for patient as well as impatient lovers, for those to whom love is a faith and sometimes a folly, for all who have fallen in love or out of it—in short for lovers past, present, and (possibly) future. Their poetry is for those who, faced with life's vexations, wish, like Omar Khayyám, to remould this sorry scheme of things nearer to the heart's desire. It is for everyone who believes with Robert Frost that:

> Earth's the right place for love:
> I don't know where it's likely to go better.

The preoccupation with love is as timeless as it is universal. As reflected in these pages it extends from antiquity to modernity. Ignoring such categories as Classical, Romantic, and Realistic, here side by side with the familiar are the not-yet-famous. The scope is from the ancient Song of Songs and Greek Anthology through Horace, Ovid, and other Latin poets, to Villon, the Medievalists, the Elizabethans, the Augustans, the Victorians, and today's contemporaries. The poems reveal the period in which they were written, yet their expression is not bound by a time or a tendency. Their moods are multiple, their emotions unpredictable, but they all speak the many-voiced language of love.

L.U.

CONTENTS

The Awakening of Love

LOVE AT FIRST SIGHT
  Christopher Marlowe   3

AWAKE! AWAKE!
  William Davenant   3

IN THE SPRING-TIME
  William Shakespeare   4

IN THE MERRY MONTH
  OF MAY   Nicholas Breton   5

TO GIVE MY LOVE
  GOOD-MORROW
    Thomas Heywood   6

THE TIME OF ROSES
  Thomas Hood   7

YOU'LL LOVE ME YET!
  Robert Browning   7

THE FIRST DAY
  Christina Rossetti   8

A WORLD STILL YOUNG
  W. E. Henley   8

A BOWL OF ROSES
  W. E. Henley   9

THE NIGHTINGALE
  W. E. Henley   9

O SWEETHEART, HEAR YOU
  James Joyce   10

IT WAS OUT BY
  DONNYCARNEY   James Joyce   10

The Enchantment of Love

BEAUTY'S SELF   Anonymous   13

BEAUTY IS NOT BOUND
  Thomas Campion   14

THE EFFECT OF LOVE
  Thomas Campion   14

SUCH SWEET NEGLECT
  Ben Jonson   15

SO WHITE, SO SOFT,
  SO SWEET   Ben Jonson   16

COME, MY CELIA   Ben Jonson   16

TO AMARANTHA
  Richard Lovelace   17

THE BRIDE   Sir John Suckling   18

GATHER YE ROSEBUDS
  Robert Herrick   19

THE BRACELET: TO JULIA
  Robert Herrick   19

TO ANTHEA, WHO MAY
  COMMAND HIM
  ANYTHING   Robert Herrick   20

UPON JULIA'S CLOTHES
  Robert Herrick   21

DELIGHT IN DISORDER
  Robert Herrick   21

THE NIGHT-PIECE: TO JULIA
  Robert Herrick   21

AWAY WITH SILKS
    Robert Herrick 22

JENNY KISSED ME   *Leigh Hunt* 23

LOVE'S SECRET   *William Blake* 23

SONG: THIS TRESS
    Robert Browning 24

YOUR KISSES   *Arthur Symons* 24

THE CHERRY-BLOSSOM
  WAND   *Anna Wickham* 25

SOMEWHERE I HAVE NEVER
  TRAVELLED   *E. E. Cummings* 26

RONDEAU   *Louis Untermeyer* 27

The Laughter of Love

THE RECONCILIATION
    Horace, Adapted by
    Louis Untermeyer 30

ALL SEASONS IN ONE
    Anonymous 31

LOVE'S LIMIT   *Anonymous* 31

O STAY, SWEET LOVE
    Anonymous 32

O, NO, JOHN   *Anonymous* 33

KISSIN'   *Anonymous* 34

THE LOVER REJOICETH
    Sir Thomas Wyatt 34

ADVICE TO A GIRL
    Thomas Campion 35

GOOD ADVICE   *Thomas Carew* 36

SIGH NO MORE
    William Shakespeare 36

CARDS FOR KISSES   *John Lyly* 37

BELINDA THE CHARITABLE
    Anonymous 37

SONG: CATCH A FALLING
  STAR   *John Donne* 38

THE THEFT   *George Wither* 40

WHAT CARE I   *George Wither* 40

THE TOUCHSTONE
    Samuel Bishop 41

UNDER THE WILLOW-
  SHADES   *William Davenant* 42

THAT FOND IMPOSSIBILITY
    Richard Lovelace 42

THE CONSTANT LOVER
    Sir John Suckling 43

WHY SO PALE AND WAN?
    Sir John Suckling 44

SWEET, LET ME GO
    William Corkine 44

"AND FORGIVE US OUR
  TRESPASSES"   *Aphra Behn* 45

MAN IS FOR THE WOMAN
  MADE   *Peter Anthony Motteaux* 45

FALSE AND FICKLE
    John Dryden 46

RESTRAINED PASSION
    Lady Mary Wortley Montagu 46

FALSE THOUGH SHE BE
    William Congreve 47

ALL OR NOTHING
    William Congreve 47

ANSWER TO JEALOUSY
    Matthew Prior 48

THE ANGRY LOVER
    Matthew Prior 49

A TRUE MAID   *Matthew Prior* 49

SONG: THE DISSEMBLER
    Matthew Prior 50

A REASONABLE AFFLICTION
    Matthew Prior 51

THE TIME I'VE LOST IN
  WOOING   *Thomas Moore* 51

BY WHAT SWEET NAME
    Samuel Taylor Coleridge 52

ADAM, LILITH, AND EVE
    Robert Browning 53

WHENEVER WE HAPPEN TO
KISS   *Heinrich Heine, Adapted
by Louis Untermeyer*   54

SUSPICIOUS SWEETHEART
*Heinrich Heine, Adapted
by Louis Untermeyer*   54

THE KISS   *Coventry Patmore*   54

WHEN I WAS ONE-AND-
TWENTY   *A. E. Housman*   55

OH, WHEN I WAS IN LOVE
WITH YOU   *A. E. Housman*   55

OH, SEE HOW THICK THE
GOLDCUP FLOWERS
A. E. Housman   56

NIGHT SONG AT AMALFI
Sara Teasdale   57

THE TIRED MAN
Anna Wickham   57

MEDITATION AT KEW
Anna Wickham   58

EQUALS   *Louis Untermeyer*   58

HOW SHE RESOLVED TO
ACT   *Merrill Moore*   59

MOURNING DOVE
Clinch Calkins   60

THAT REMINDS ME
Ogden Nash   61

A SUBALTERN'S LOVE-SONG
John Betjeman   62

TRUE LOVE   *Judith Viorst*   63

CAPSULE CONCLUSIONS
Old German Proverbs   64

RONDEL OF MERCILESS
BEAUTY   *Geoffrey Chaucer*   70

ROUNDEL OF FAREWELL
*François Villon, Translated
by John Payne*   71

THE FORSAKEN LOVER
Sir Thomas Wyatt   71

WITH HOW SAD STEPS, O
MOON   *Sir Philip Sidney*   72

SINCE THERE'S NO HELP
Michael Drayton   73

SHE NEVER TOLD HER
LOVE   *William Shakespeare*   73

SEALS OF LOVE
William Shakespeare   74

GREENSLEEVES
Clement Robinson   74

KIND ARE HER ANSWERS
Thomas Campion   75

BREAK OF DAY   *John Donne*   76

SWEETEST LOVE, I DO NOT
GO   *John Donne*   76

SONG: HOW SWEET I
ROAMED   *William Blake*   77

THE GARDEN OF LOVE
William Blake   78

THE BANKS O' DOON
Robert Burns   79

AE FOND KISS   *Robert Burns*   80

I CRY YOUR MERCY
John Keats   81

WE'LL GO NO MORE
A-ROVING   *George Gordon,
Lord Byron*   81

WHEN WE TWO PARTED
*George Gordon,
Lord Byron*   82

FAREWELL!   *George Gordon,
Lord Byron*   83

A DREAM WITHIN A
DREAM   *Edgar Allan Poe*   83

MOTHER, I CANNOT MIND
MY WHEEL
Walter Savage Landor   84

The
Pain
of Love

LOVE HAVE I BORNE MUCH
*Ovid, Translated by
Christopher Marlowe*   68

IN LOVE WITH TWO
*Ovid, Translated by
Christopher Marlowe*   69

ASK ME NO MORE
　　　　　Alfred Tennyson 85

THE SOUL SELECTS HER
　OWN SOCIETY
　　　　　Emily Dickinson 86

I HAVE NO LIFE BUT THIS
　　　　　Emily Dickinson 86

COME SLOWLY, EDEN!
　　　　　Emily Dickinson 86

I CANNOT LIVE WITH
　YOU　　　Emily Dickinson 87

OF ALL THE SOULS THAT
　STAND CREATE
　　　　　Emily Dickinson 88

MINE　　　Emily Dickinson 89

WILD NIGHTS!
　　　　　Emily Dickinson 89

MY LIFE CLOSED TWICE
　　　　　Emily Dickinson 89

THE HOPE I DREAMED OF
　　　　　Christina Rossetti 90

REMEMBER ME
　　　　　Christina Rossetti 90

SONG: WHEN I AM DEAD
　　　　　Christina Rossetti 91

ECHO　　Christina Rossetti 91

A FAREWELL
　　　　　Coventry Patmore 92

THE MARRIED LOVER
　　　　　Coventry Patmore 93

NEUTRAL TONES
　　　　　Thomas Hardy 94

SING, BALLAD-SINGER
　　　　　Thomas Hardy 94

JUNE　　　Amy Levy 95

LESS THAN THE DUST
　　　　　Laurence Hope 96

FAITHFUL IN MY FASHION
　　　　　Ernest Dowson 97

WHEN YOU ARE OLD
　　　　William Butler Yeats 98

WHITE IN THE MOON
　　　　A. E. Housman 98

BREDON HILL　A. E. Housman 99

SEA LOVE　　Charlotte Mew 100

I HAVE BEEN THROUGH
　THE GATES　Charlotte Mew 101

LOVE SONG FROM NEW
　ENGLAND　Winifred Welles 101

WHAT LIPS MY LIPS HAVE
　KISSED
　　　Edna St. Vincent Millay 102

FOLK-SONG　Louis Untermeyer 102

STOP ALL THE CLOCKS
　　　　　W. H. Auden 103

LOVE 20¢ THE FIRST
　QUARTER MILE
　　　　Kenneth Fearing 104

MEMENTOS　W. D. Snodgrass 105

ELEGY FOR A MIS-SPENT
　YOUTH　Jon Stallworthy 106

FINIS?　　Michael Lewis 106

The
Drama
of Love

LORD RANDAL　Anonymous 108

THE DOUGLAS TRAGEDY
　　　　　Anonymous 109

BARBARA ALLEN　Anonymous 112

THE LOST MISTRESS
　　　　Robert Browning 113

TWO IN THE CAMPAGNA
　　　　Robert Browning 114

MEETING AT NIGHT
　　　　Robert Browning 115

PORPHYRIA'S LOVER
　　　　Robert Browning 116

MUCKLE-MOUTH MEG
　　　　Robert Browning 118

IS MY TEAM PLOUGHING?
A. E. Housman 119

DOVER BEACH
Matthew Arnold 120

THE TRUE LOVER
A. E. Housman 121

LOVE ON THE FARM
D. H. Lawrence 122

THE FIRED POT
Anna Wickham 125

IMPERIAL ADAM   A. D. Hope 126

The Fulfillment of Love

LOVE'S CONSTANCY
Anonymous 129

YOU   Anonymous 130

BALLADE OF THE WOMEN
OF PARIS
François Villon, Translated by
Algernon Charles Swinburne 130

BALLADE FOR A
BRIDEGROOM
François Villon, Translated by
Algernon Charles Swinburne 131

MY TRUE-LOVE HATH MY
HEART   Sir Philip Sidney 132

SEND BACK MY HEART
Sir John Suckling 132

TO ALTHEA FROM PRISON
Richard Lovelace 133

MY LIGHT THOU ART
John Wilmot, Earl of Rochester 134

MY HEART AT REST
Sir Charles Sedley 135

FULFILLMENT
William Cavendish 135

I SHALL HAVE HAD MY
DAY   Alfred Tennyson 137

A BIRTHDAY   Christina Rossetti 137

SILENT NOON
Dante Gabriel Rossetti 138

RENOUNCEMENT
Alice Meynell 139

ROMANCE
Robert Louis Stevenson 139

THE DARK CHAMBER
Louis Untermeyer 140

TO A WEEPING WILLOW
Louis Untermeyer 141

SINCE I SAW MY LOVE
Anna Wickham 142

THE MAN WITH A
HAMMER   Anna Wickham 142

"NOT MARBLE, NOR THE
GILDED MONUMENTS"
Archibald MacLeish 143

BALLADE   Karl Shapiro 144

WINTER TRYST
Ormonde de Kay, Jr. 145

ALL THE TREE'S HANDS
Jeannette Nichols 146

THE WIFE   Denise Levertov 147

CRYSTAL ANNIVERSARY
Philip Appleman 148

DAY DREAM   Nancy Cardozo 149

The Gallantry of Love

MORE THAN MOST FAIR
Edmund Spenser 151

FEAR NOT, DEAR LOVE
Thomas Carew 152

DRINK TO ME ONLY WITH
THINE EYES   Ben Jonson 152

TO LUCASTA, ON GOING TO
THE WARS   Richard Lovelace 153

O WERT THOU IN THE
CAULD BLAST   *Robert Burns* 154

SWEET AFTON   *Robert Burns* 154

The Ecstasy of Love

BEHOLD, THOU ART FAIR
The Song of Songs 157

O WESTERN WIND
Anonymous 160

THERE IS A LADY
Anonymous 160

SO FAST ENTANGLED
Anonymous 160

THE SUN RISING   *John Donne* 161

GO, LOVELY ROSE!
Edmund Waller 162

ASK ME NO MORE
Thomas Carew 163

ON A GIRDLE   *Edmund Waller* 164

A RED, RED ROSE
Robert Burns 165

TO DREAM OF THEE
John Keats 165

THE INDIAN SERENADE
Percy Bysshe Shelley 166

SHE WALKS IN BEAUTY
George Gordon, Lord Byron 166

HOW MANY TIMES?
Thomas Lovell Beddoes 167

AN ARAB LOVE-SONG
Francis Thompson 168

TO HELEN   *Edgar Allan Poe* 168

PRESS CLOSE BARE-BOSOM'D
NIGHT   *Walt Whitman* 169

LOVE: TWO VIGNETTES
Robert Penn Warren 169

THE HILL   *Rupert Brooke* 171

The Urgency of Love

FROM "THE GREEK
ANTHOLOGY"
Adapted by Louis Untermeyer 173

LET US LIVE AND LOVE
*Catullus, Adapted by
Thomas Campion* 175

MY LIFE'S DELIGHT
Thomas Campion 175

WHEN WE COURT AND
KISS   *Thomas Campion* 176

FOLLOW YOUR SAINT
Thomas Campion 177

MORE LOVE OR MORE
DISDAIN   *Thomas Carew* 177

TO A LADY ASKING HIM
HOW LONG HE WOULD
LOVE HER
Sir George Etherege 178

THE PASSIONATE SHEPHERD
TO HIS LOVE
Christopher Marlowe 179

MARRIAGE OF TRUE MINDS
William Shakespeare 180

FORTUNE AND MEN'S EYES
William Shakespeare 181

SHALL I COMPARE THEE?
William Shakespeare 181

DEVOURING TIME
William Shakespeare 182

HOW LIKE A WINTER
William Shakespeare 182

WHEN MY LOVE SWEARS
William Shakespeare 183

FAREWELL!
William Shakespeare 183

O MISTRESS MINE
William Shakespeare 183

WHY SHOULD WE DELAY?
Edmund Waller 184

HER HEART
Bartholomew Griffin 185

XV

TO HIS COY MISTRESS
    Andrew Marvell 185

LOVE WILL FIND OUT THE
    WAY   *Anonymous* 187

WHISTLE AN' I'LL COME
    Robert Burns 188

LOVE'S PHILOSOPHY
    Percy Bysshe Shelley 189

I KNOW WHO I LOVE
    Anonymous 189

A WOMAN'S LAST WORD
    Robert Browning 190

THE MOTH'S KISS, FIRST!
    Robert Browning 191

IN LOVE, IF LOVE BE LOVE
    Alfred Tennyson 192

NOW SLEEPS THE CRIMSON
    PETAL   *Alfred Tennyson* 192

NOW!   *Robert Browning* 193

HEART'S DESIRE
    Omar Khayyam-Fitzgerald 193

PARFUM EXOTIQUE
    Charles Baudelaire, Translated by
    Arthur Symons 194

YOUR KISSES   *Arthur Symons* 194

LOVE AND SLEEP
    Algernon Charles Swinburne 195

SONG
    Algernon Charles Swinburne 195

IN MAY   *J. M. Synge* 196

THE TIRED WOMAN
    Anna Wickham 197

I KNEW A WOMAN
    Theodore Roethke 197

TRAVEL   *Leonard Cohen* 199

DECEMBER 18th   *Anne Sexton* 199

The Mystery of Love

I HEAR SOME SAY
    Michael Drayton 202

WHEN MEN SHALL FIND
    THY FLOWER *Samuel Daniel* 203

MUSIC, WHEN SOFT VOICES
    DIE   *Percy Bysshe Shelley* 203

BRIGHT STAR   *John Keats* 204

LOVE-SONG *Rainer Maria Rilke* 204

HOW DO I LOVE THEE?
    Elizabeth Barrett Browning 205

IF THOU MUST LOVE ME
    Elizabeth Barrett Browning 205

WHEN OUR TWO SOULS
    STAND UP
    Elizabeth Barrett Browning 206

SUDDEN LIGHT
    Dante Gabriel Rossetti 207

TO ONE IN PARADISE
    Edgar Allan Poe 207

THE SILKEN TENT
    Robert Frost 208

THE NIGHT HAS A
    THOUSAND EYES
    Francis William Bourdillon 209

A VIRGINAL   *Ezra Pound* 209

FOR MIRIAM *Kenneth Patchen* 210

THE LOVERS   *Conrad Aiken* 211

The
Awakening
of
Love

Falling in love may happen as suddenly as a rapt revelation or as gradually as an opening flower. "Who ever loved that loved not at first sight?" exclaims Christopher Marlowe. Thomas Hood vividly remembers the sensation:

> . . . the world was newly crowned
> With flowers, when first we met.

while Christina Rossetti tries to recollect the unrecorded event:

> I wish I could remember the first day,
> First hour, first moment of your meeting me;

The awakening of love is a unique emotional experience; indeed it is sometimes unrecognizable. It cannot be explained any more than one can explain the coming of spring or the conviction which Herrick has expressed for every lover's delight in his devotion:

> Thou art my life, my love, my heart,
>   The very eyes of me;
> Thou hast command of every part
>   To live and die for thee.

When love wakes it transforms the world with surprises. It is the time of roses, of dalliance, of happy innocence and, at the same time, the beginning of knowledge. "A poem," said Robert Frost, "begins in delight and ends in wisdom. The figure is the same for love. . . . It is the surprise of remembering something we didn't know we knew."

The lover may not always recall love's awakening, but he can never wholly forget it. The poet remembers it—and says it—for him.

His sixteenth-century fellow-poets referred to Christopher Marlowe as "the Muses' Darling." Ben Jonson praised his "mighty line," and, three hundred years after his death, Swinburne hailed him "crowned, girdled, garbed and shod with light and fire." Killed in a tavern brawl before he was thirty, Marlowe left four plays filled with rhetorical exuberance—all of them written within six years—besides one of the most imitated of Elizabethan lyrics, "The Passionate Shepherd to His Love" (see page 179), and a long uncompleted erotic narrative poem, "Hero and Leander," from which the following excerpt is taken.

LOVE AT FIRST SIGHT

It lies not in our power to love or hate,
For will in us is over-ruled by fate.
When two are stripped, long ere the course begin
We wish that one should lose, the other win;
And one especially do we affect
Of two gold ingots, like in each respect.
The reason no man knows; let it suffice,
What we behold is censured by our eyes.
Where both deliberate, the love is slight;
Who ever loved, that loved not at first sight?

Christopher Marlowe

William Davenant was famous for two things. He was England's second poet laureate, and he was rumored to be an illegitimate son of Shakespeare. Although a minor poet and dramatist, he was buried with great ceremony in Westminster Abbey.

Davenant's mischievous "Under the Willow-Shades" is on page 42.

AWAKE! AWAKE!

The lark now leaves his watery nest,
    And, climbing, shakes his dewy wings.
He takes this window for the East,
    And to implore your light he sings—
Awake! awake! The morn will never rise
Till she can dress her beauty at your eyes.

The merchant bows unto the seaman's star,
    The ploughman from the sun his season takes;
But still the lover wonders what they are
    Who look for day before his mistress wakes.
Awake! awake! Break through your veils of lawn!
Then draw your curtains, and begin the dawn!

William Davenant

Shakespeare's As You Like It *is a woodland comedy, an idyl that is buoyant with country songs. Here is one of the most tuneful of them, a four-hundred-year-old ditty which is still sung today.*

IN THE SPRING-TIME

It was a lover and his lass,
  With a hey, and a ho, and a hey nonino,
That o'er the green corn-field did pass
  In the spring-time, the only pretty ring-time,
When birds do sing, hey ding a ding, ding;
  Sweet lovers love the spring.

Between the acres of the rye,
  With a hey, and a ho, and a hey nonino,
These pretty country folks would lie,
  In the spring-time, the only pretty ring-time,
When birds do sing, hey ding a ding, ding;
  Sweet lovers love the spring.

This carol they began that hour,
  With a hey, and a ho, and a hey nonino,
How that a life was but a flower
  In the spring-time, the only pretty ring-time,
When birds do sing, hey ding a ding, ding;
  Sweet lovers love the spring.

And therefore take the present time,
  With a hey, and a ho, and a hey nonino,
For love is crownèd with the prime
  In the spring-time, the only pretty ring-time,
When birds do sing, hey ding a ding, ding;
  Sweet lovers love the spring.

William Shakespeare

All of Nicholas Breton's many moral pamphlets are forgotten, but his pretty pastoral songs continue to be anthologized. Several of them appeared in England's Helicon (*1600*) and immediately became popular because (or even though) they were, according to a modern commentator, "remarkably free of grossness."

IN THE MERRY MONTH OF MAY

In the merry month of May,
In a morn by break of day
Forth I walked by the wood-side,
When as May was in his pride.
There I spiéd, all alone,
Phyllida and Corydon.
Much ado there was, God wot,
He would love and she would not.
She said, "Never man was true."
He said, "None was false to you."
He said he had loved her long.
She said, "Love should have no wrong."
Corydon would kiss her then.
She said maids must kiss no men
Till they did for good and all.
Then she made the shepherd call
All the heavens to witness truth,
Never loved a truer youth.
Thus, with many a pretty oath,
Yea and nay, and faith and troth,
Such as silly shepherds use
When they will not love abuse,
Love which had been long deluded
Was with kisses sweet concluded.
And Phyllida with garlands gay
Was made the lady of the May.

Nicholas Breton

An actor-playwright, Thomas Heywood turned out dozens of dramas, many of which are irretrievably—some critics say fortunately—lost. Charles Lamb mingled praise and criticism when he called Heywood "a prose Shakespeare."

TO GIVE MY LOVE GOOD-MORROW

Pack, clouds, away! and welcome, day!
  With night we banish sorrow.
Sweet air, blow soft; mount, lark, aloft
  To give my Love good-morrow!
Wings from the wind to please her mind,
  Notes from the lark I'll borrow:
Bird, prune thy wing! nightingale, sing!
  To give my Love good-morrow!
  To give my Love good-morrow,
  Notes from them all I'll borrow.

Wake from thy nest, robin red-breast!
  Sing, birds, in every furrow!
And from each bill let music shrill
  Give my fair Love good-morrow!
Blackbird and thrush in every bush,
  Stare, linnet, and cock-sparrow,
You pretty elves, amongst yourselves,
  Sing my fair Love good-morrow!
  To give my Love good-morrow,
  Sing, birds, in every furrow!

Thomas Heywood

Thomas Hood wrote some of the most serious and some of the most humorous, pun-crowded, nonsensical verses of the nineteenth century. His range was extraordinarily wide, from the violently melodramatic "The Dream of Eugene Aram" to the socially conscious "The Song of the Shirt" and occasional lyrics as tenderly graceful as "The Time of Roses."

THE TIME OF ROSES

It was not in the winter
Our loving lot was cast:
It was the time of roses—
We plucked them as we passed!

That churlish season never frowned
On early lovers yet!
O, no—the world was newly crowned
With flowers, when first we met.

'Twas twilight, and I bade you go,
But still you held me fast:
It was the time of roses—
We plucked them as we passed.

Thomas Hood

YOU'LL LOVE ME YET!

You'll love me yet! And I can tarry
    Your love's protracted growing.
June reared that bunch of flowers you carry
    From seeds of April's sowing.

I plant a heartful now; some seed
    At least is sure to strike
And yield—what you'll not pluck indeed,
    Not love, but, may be, like.

You'll look at least on love's remains,
    A grave's one violet.
Your look?—that pays a thousand pains—
    What's death! You'll love me yet!

Robert Browning

7

The Rossettis were a particularly gifted family. Dante Gabriel was a painter, poet, and leader of the group known as the Pre-Raphaelites; William Michael was a biographer, critic, and editor; Christina Georgina was an eminent sonneteer and an exquisite lyricist. Other poems by Christina, the youngest and most ascetic of the Rossettis, are on pages 90, 91, and 137.

THE FIRST DAY

I wish I could remember the first day,
First hour, first moment of your meeting me;
If bright or dim the season, it might be
Summer or winter for aught I can say.
So unrecorded did it slip away,
So blind was I to see and to foresee,
So dull to mark the budding of my tree
That would not blossom yet for many a May.

If only I could recollect it! Such
A day of days! I let it come and go
As traceless as a thaw of bygone snow.
It seemed to mean so little, meant so much!
If only now I could recall that touch,
First touch of hand in hand!—Did one but know!

Christina Rossetti

The classroom has identified Henley with "I am the master of my fate / I am the captain of my soul." But "Invictus" is not Henley's only claim to be quoted. His "London Voluntaries" were experiments in a new form before free verse became fashionable, and his songs show, as he said, that "the lyrical instinct had slept, not died."

A WORLD STILL YOUNG

In the red April dawn,
   In the wild April weather,
From brake and thicket and lawn,
   The birds sang together.

The look of the hoyden Spring
    Is pinched and shrewish and cold;
But all together they sing
    Of a world that can never be old:

Of a world still young—still young!—
    Whose last word won't be said,
Nor her last song dreamed and sung
    Till her last true lover's dead.

                  W. E. Henley

A BOWL OF ROSES

It was a bowl of roses;
    There in the light they lay,
Languishing, glorying, glowing
    Their life away.

And the soul of them, like a presence,
    Into me crept and grew,
And filled me with something—someone—
    O, was it you?

                  W. E. Henley

THE NIGHTINGALE

The nightingale has a lyre of gold,
    The lark's is a clarion call,
And the blackbird plays but a boxwood flute,
    But I love him best of all.

For his song is all of the joy of life,
    And we in the mad, spring weather,
We two have listened till he sang
    Our hearts and lips together.

                  W. E. Henley

Long before James Joyce wrote the panoramic Ulysses and the monumental language experiment, Finnegans Wake, he was writing conventional poetry. He was twenty-five when his first book, Chamber Music, was published; in it Joyce echoed not only the early Irishry of William Butler Yeats but strains of various Elizabethan poets.

O SWEETHEART, HEAR YOU

O sweetheart, hear you
   Your lover's tale;
A man shall have sorrow
   When friends him fail.

For he shall know then
   Friends be untrue
And a little ashes
   Their words come to.

But one unto him
   Will softly move
And softly woo him
   In ways of love.

His hand is under
   Her smooth round breast;
So he who has sorrow
   Shall have rest.

James Joyce

IT WAS OUT BY DONNYCARNEY

O, it was out by Donnycarney,
   When the bat flew from tree to tree,
My love and I did walk together,
   And sweet were the words she said to me.

Along with us the summer wind
   Went murmuring—O, happily!—
But softer than the breath of summer
   Was the kiss she gave to me.

James Joyce

The
Enchantment
of
Love

Milton's Comus *is almost breathless with wonder when, for the first time, he sees his Lady:*

> Can any mortal mixture of earth's mould
> Breathe such divine enchanting ravishment!

Thus lovers fall under the spell of love's radiance and what Thomas Moore called "those endearing young charms." The enchantment is epitomized by Richard Lovelace when he bids his Amarantha to shake her head "and scatter day," by Ben Jonson when he compares his beloved to a bright lily "before rude hands have touched it" and the new-fallen snow "before the soil hath smutched it," by Robert Herrick who is spellbound by the rustle of Julia's silks and "the liquefaction of her clothes," by Anna Wickham who, in "The Cherry-Blossom Wand," summons the magic and mystical bewitchment of "a beautiful thing that can never grow wise." And it is glorified by George Bernard Shaw in the prose poetry of Mrs. George, the clairvoyant Mayoress, in Shaw's Getting Married:

> "When you loved me I gave you the whole sun and stars
> to play with. I gave you eternity in a single moment,
> strength of the mountains in one clasp of your arms, and
> the volume of all the seas in one impulse of your soul . . .
> We possessed all the universe together."

It is this enchantment of love that makes all lovers clasp "eternity in a single moment" and possess "all the universe together."

BEAUTY'S SELF

My love in her attire doth show her wit,
    It doth so well become her:
For every season she hath dressings fit,
    For winter, spring, and summer.
No beauty she doth miss
    When all her robes are on;
But Beauty's self she is
    When all her robes are gone.

Anonymous

BEAUTY IS NOT BOUND

Give beauty all her right!
She's not to one form tied;
Each shape yields fair delight
Where her perfections bide:
Helen, I grant, might pleasing be,
And Rosamond was as sweet as she.

Some the quick eye commends,
Some swelling lips and red;
Pale looks have many friends,
Through sacred sweetness bred:
Meadows have flowers that pleasures move,
Though roses are the flowers of love.

Free beauty is not bound
To one unmovéd clime;
She visits every ground
And favors every time.
Let the old loves with mine compare;
My sovereign is as sweet and fair.

Thomas Campion

THE EFFECT OF LOVE

Other beauties others move;
    In you I all graces find.
Such is the effect of love,
    To make them happy that are kind.

Sweet, afford me then your sight
    That, surveying all your looks,
Endless volumes I may write
    And fill the world with envied books,

Which, when after-ages view,
    All shall wonder and despair:
Women to find a man so true,
    Or men a woman half so fair.

Thomas Campion

14

Cherished by Shakespeare, who acted in one of his plays, idolized by young poets who called themselves "the tribe of Ben," Ben Jonson was favored by three monarchs. Queen Elizabeth delighted in his comedies; James I persuaded him to turn from tragedies to masques; Charles I made him England's first poet laureate. After a lustily expansive life, he was buried in Westminster Abbey, and this terse but significant tribute was cut into his tombstone: "O rare Ben Jonson."

SUCH SWEET NEGLECT

Still to be neat, still to be drest
As you were going to a feast:
Still to be powdered, still perfumed:
Lady, it is to be presumed,
Though art's hid causes are not found,
All is not sweet, all is not sound.

Give me a look, give me a face
That makes simplicity a grace;
Robes loosely flowing, hair as free:
Such sweet neglect more taketh me,
Than all the adulteries of art,
That strike mine eyes, but not my heart.

Ben Jonson

SO WHITE, SO SOFT, SO SWEET

Have you seen but a bright lily grow
 Before rude hands have touched it?
Have you marked but the fall of the snow
 Before the soil hath smutched it?
Have you felt the wool of the beaver,
 Or swan's down ever?
Or have smelt o' the bud of the brier,
 Or the nard[1] in the fire?
Or have tasted the bag of the bee?
O so white, O so soft, O so sweet is she!

Ben Jonson

COME, MY CELIA

Come, my Celia, let us prove,
While we can, the sports of love.
Time will not be ours for ever;
He, at length, our good will sever.
Spend not then his gifts in vain:
Suns that set may rise again.
But if once we lose this light,
'Tis with us perpetual night.
Why should we defer our joys?
Fame and rumor are but toys.
Cannot we delude the eyes
Of a few poor household spies?
Or his easier ears beguile,
Thus removéd by our wile?
'Tis no sin love's fruits to steal,
But the sweet thefts to reveal;
To be taken, to be seen,
These have crimes accounted been.

Ben Jonson

The names of Lovelace and Suckling are paired almost as often as those of Shelley and Keats. Both were nobly born, both were knighted by James I, and both lived adventurous lives. Both, alas, ended tragically. Suckling died at thirty-three—it has never been established whether

[1]Nard: spikenard, an aromatic oil used as incense.

he committed suicide or was stabbed by a treacherous servant; Lovelace lived to be forty but, always in trouble, died, poverty-stricken, in a foul cellar.

Besides two of their poems which follow, six others are on pages 42-44, 132, 133, and 153.

TO AMARANTHA

THAT SHE WOULD DISHEVEL HER HAIR

Amarantha, sweet and fair,
Ah, braid no more that shining hair!
As my curious hand or eye
Hovering round thee, let it fly!

Let it fly as unconfined
As its calm ravisher, the wind,
Who hath left his darling East
To wanton o'er that spicy nest.

Every tress must be confessed,
But neatly tangled at the best;
Like a clue of golden thread
Most excellently ravelléd.

Do not, then, wind up that light
In ribbands, and o'ercloud in night,
Like the Sun in's early ray;
But shake your head, and scatter day!

Richard Lovelace

THE BRIDE
(From "A Ballad Upon a Wedding")

Her feet beneath her petticoat,
Like little mice, stole in and out,
   As if they fear'd the light:
But O she dances such a way!
   No sun upon an Easter-day
   Is half so fine a sight.

Her finger was so small, the ring
Would not stay on, which they did bring,
   It was too wide a peck:
And to say truth (for out it must)
It looked like the great collar, just,
   About our young colt's neck.

Her cheeks so rare a white was on,
No daisy makes comparison;
   Who sees them is undone;
For streaks of red were mingled there,
Such as are on a Catherine pear,
   The side that's next the sun.

Her lips were red, and one was thin,
Compar'd to that was next her chin
   (Some bee had stung it newly);
But, Dick, her eyes so guard her face;
I durst no more upon them gaze
   Than on the sun in July.

Sir John Suckling

   The seventeenth-century Robert Herrick wrote some of the nimblest and some of the naughtiest poetry of his day. As a vicar he composed Noble Numbers or Pious Pieces, but this did not stop his celebrations of the lush, lawless beauty of nature and the flow of frankly pagan love lyrics. In grace and exquisite miniature painting Herrick is unexcelled; no one has surpassed him in his sense of ease and seemingly offhand spontaneity. More than any other poet he trifled his way from light verse to pure poetry. Immortal are the love-inspired lines which begin "Gather ye rosebuds while ye may," "Bid me to live, and I will live,"

"Whenas in silks my Julia goes," and "A sweet disorder in the dress."
Such poems can never lose their fragrance—they perfume the page on
which they are printed.

GATHER YE ROSEBUDS

Gather ye rosebuds while ye may,
　Old Time is still a-flying;
And this same flower that smiles today
　Tomorrow will be dying.

The glorious lamp of heaven, the Sun,
　The higher he's a-getting,
The sooner will his race be run,
　And nearer he's to setting.

That age is best, which is the first,
　When youth and blood are warmer
But being spent, the worse, and worst
　Times still succeed the former.

Then be not coy, but use your time,
　And while you may, go marry:
For having lost but once your prime,
　You may for ever tarry.

Robert Herrick

THE BRACELET: TO JULIA

Why I tie about thy wrist,
Julia, this my silken twist;
For what other reason is't,
But to show thee how in part
Thou my pretty captive art?
But thy bond-slave is my heart.
'Tis but silk that bindeth thee,
Snap the thread and thou art free:
But 'tis otherwise with me;
I am bound, and fast bound so
That from thee I cannot go;
If I could, I would not so.

Robert Herrick

TO ANTHEA, WHO MAY COMMAND
HIM ANYTHING

Bid me to live, and I will live
 Thy protestant to be;
Or bid me love, and I will give
 A loving heart to thee.

A heart as soft, a heart as kind,
 A heart as sound and free
As in the whole world thou canst find,
 That heart I'll give to thee.

Bid that heart stay, and it will stay
 To honor thy decree:
Or bid it languish quite away,
 And 't shall do so for thee.

Bid me to weep, and I will weep
 While I have eyes to see:
And, having none, yet will I keep
 A heart to weep for thee.

Bid me despair; and I'll despair
 Under that cypress-tree:
Or bid me die, and I will dare
 E'en death to die for thee.

Thou art my life, my love, my heart,
 The very eyes of me:
And hast command of every part
 To live and die for thee.

Robert Herrick

UPON JULIA'S CLOTHES

Whenas in silks my Julia goes
Then, then (methinks) how sweetly flows
That liquefaction of her clothes.

Next, when I cast mine eyes and see
That brave vibration each way free;
O how that glittering taketh me!

Robert Herrick

DELIGHT IN DISORDER

A sweet disorder in the dress
Kindles in clothes a wantonness:
A lawn about the shoulders thrown
Into a fine distractión,
An erring lace, which here and there
Enthralls the crimson stomacher,
A cuff neglectful, and thereby
Ribbands to flow confusedly,
A winning wave (deserving note)
In the tempestuous petticoat,
A careless shoe-string, in whose tie
I see a wild civility,
Do more bewitch me, than when art
Is too precise in every part.

Robert Herrick

THE NIGHT-PIECE: TO JULIA

Her eyes the glow-worm lend thee;
The shooting stars attend thee;
    And the elves also,
    Whose little eyes glow
Like the sparks of fire, befriend thee.

No will-o'-th'-wisp mislight thee,
Nor snake or slow-worm bite thee;
    But on, on thy way,
    Not making a stay,
Since ghost there's none to affright thee.

Let not the dark thee cumber;
What though the moon does slumber?
    The stars of the night
    Will lend thee their light
Like tapers clear, without number.

Then, Julia, let me woo thee,
Thus, thus, to come unto me;
    And when I shall meet
    Thy silvery feet,
My soul I'll pour into thee.

Robert Herrick

AWAY WITH SILKS

Away with silks, away with lawn;
I'll have no screens or curtains drawn.
Give me my mistress as she is,
Dressed in her nak'd simplicities.
For as my heart, e'en so my eye
Is won with flesh, not drapery.

Robert Herrick

Son of a conservative clergyman, Leigh Hunt was always doing surprising things. He called the Prince Regent "a fat Adonis of fifty," and as a consequence was imprisoned for two years. He flaunted public opinion by going to Italy with Byron and publishing a journal called The Liberal there. A friend of Keats, he challenged him to a sonnet composition, the subject being "The Grasshopper and the Cricket." Hunt's first line was "Green little vaulter in the sunny grass"; Keats' was the unforgettable "The poetry of earth is never dead." Of Hunt's hundreds of poems, the one which has outlived all the others is the bright little "Jenny Kissed Me."

JENNY KISSED ME

Jenny kissed me when we met,
Jumping from the chair she sat in;
Time, you thief, who love to get
Sweets into your list, put that in!
Say I'm weary, say I'm sad,
Say that health and wealth have missed me,
Say I'm growing old, but add,
Jenny kissed me.

Leigh Hunt

The magnificent simplicities of Blake's Songs of Innocence, which read as though they were composed impromptu by an inspired child, were followed by the heavier and more intellectual Songs of Experience. "Love's Secret" is a cross between Blake's early, innocent imagination and a later, darker vision.

LOVE'S SECRET

Never seek to tell thy love,
Love that never told can be;
For the gentle wind does move
Silently, invisibly.

I told my love, I told my love,
I told her all my heart; ✓
Trembling, cold, in ghastly fears.
Ah! she did depart!

Soon as she was gone from me
A traveler came by.
Silently, invisibly,
He took her with a sigh.

William Blake

Robert Browning was a little-known poet in his early thirties when he met Elizabeth Barrett, a popular poet of thirty-nine. Their romance is one of literature's great love stories. During the courtship she sent him a lock of her hair. The gift found its response in Browning's "Song" with its conviction that earth held nothing "above this tress."

Other poems by Browning are on pages 7, 53, 113-118, 190, 191, and 193.

SONG: THIS TRESS

Nay, but you, who do not love her,
   Is she not pure gold, my mistress?
Holds earth aught—speak truth—above her?
   Aught like this tress, see, and this tress,
And this last fairest tress of all,
So fair, see, ere I let it fall?

Because, you spend your lives in praising;
   To praise, you search the wide world over:
So, why not witness, calmly gazing,
   If earth hold aught—speak truth—above her?
Above this tress, and this I touch
But cannot praise, I love so much!

Robert Browning

During the 1890s, Arthur Symons was a leader of the Symbolist Movement and became identified with the so-called Fleshly School, or Deadly Nightshade flowering of erotic verse. "Your Kisses" is typical of his style as well as the style of his period.

For another poem by Symons see page 194.

YOUR KISSES

Sweet, can I sing you the song of your kisses?
How soft is this one, how subtle this is;
How fluttering swift as a bird's kiss that is,
As a bird that taps at a leafy lattice;
How this one clings, and how that uncloses
From bud to flower in the way of roses;
And this through laughter, and that through weeping
Swims to the brim where Love lies sleeping;

And this in a pout I snatch, and capture
That in an ecstasy of rapture,
When the odorous red-rose petals part
That my lips may find their way to the heart
Of the rose of the world, your lips, my rose.
But no song knows
The way of my heart to the heart of my rose.

Arthur Symons

It has been said that Anna Wickham wrote the way D. H. Lawrence might have written had he been a woman. Sometimes her lyrics carry musical overtones of Yeats, but the poignance is her own. For the most part she mirrors the nervous tension of the times in her wry compromises between the desire for perfection and the knowledge of its inevitable frustration. Her poetry cries out:

> Let it be something for my song,
> If it is sometimes swift and strong.

Other poems by Anna Wickham are on pages 57, 58, 125, 142, and 197.

THE CHERRY-BLOSSOM WAND

I will pluck from my tree a cherry-blossom wand,
And carry it in my merciless hand,
So I will drive you, so bewitch your eyes,
With a beautiful thing that can never grow wise.

Light are the petals that fall from the bough,
And lighter the love that I offer you now;
In a spring day shall the tale be told
Of the beautiful things that will never grow old.

The blossoms shall fall in the night wind,
And I will leave you so, to be kind:
Eternal in beauty are short-lived flowers,
Eternal in beauty, these exquisite hours.

I will pluck from my tree a cherry-blossom wand,
And carry it in my merciless hand,
So I will drive you, so bewitch your eyes,
With a beautiful thing that shall never grow wise.

Anna Wickham

E. E. Cummings *wrote more than seven hundred poems, most of which were broken into facets without punctuation or with punctuation where no reader would expect to find it. There was no question but that Cummings had found new ways of saying old things. His most eccentric typography could not conceal the sensitive, and even sentimental, romanticist.*

SOMEWHERE I HAVE NEVER TRAVELLED

somewhere i have never travelled, gladly beyond
any experience, your eyes have their silence:
in your most frail gesture are things which enclose me,
or which i cannot touch because they are too near

your slightest look easily will unclose me
though i have closed myself as fingers,
you open always petal by petal myself as Spring opens
(touching skilfully, mysteriously) her first rose

or if your wish be to close me, i and
my life will shut very beautifully, suddenly,
as when the heart of this flower imagines
the snow carefully everywhere descending;

nothing which we are to perceive in this world equals
the power of your intense fragility: whose texture
compels me with the color of its countries,
rendering death and forever with each breathing

(i do not know what it is about you that closes
and opens; only something in me understands
the voice of your eyes is deeper than all roses)
nobody, not even the rain, has such small hands

E. E. Cummings

*This, which follows, is a pouring of new wine into an old bottle, a
contemporary setting framed in an ancient French form.*

RONDEAU

Do you recall what I recall?
It was a night in early fall,
    Windless, with just a touch of chill.
    We scarcely knew each other. Still
We laughed at things conventional.

    There was the room, shabby and small:
    A chair, a couch, an empty wall,
        A lone plant on the window-sill.
            Do you recall?

    Nothing to cherish or enthrall;
    Barren of beauty as a stall;
        Yet there we stood entranced, until
        We felt the night press close and fill
    Our lives with nothing less than all . . .
            Do you recall?

Louis Untermeyer

The
Laughter
of
Love

In the wide domain of love there is room for laughter. Poems about the folly of love are almost as common as those celebrating its fulfillment. Sometimes the laughter is light and playful, sometimes it is mocking and sharpened with irony. Nowhere is the battle of the sexes waged more determinedly and comically than in the lyrics in which women accuse all men of being deceivers, and men reply that all women are either unresponsive or unfaithful. Alexander Pope bitterly assails "the fair sex" with:

> Men, some to business, some to pleasure take;
> But every woman is at heart a rake.

The frolicsome John Gay—he of The Beggar's Opera—goes further than Pope with:

> Men may escape from rope and gun;
>   Nay, some have outlived the doctor's pill;
> Who takes a woman must be undone,
>   That basilisk is sure to kill.

Earlier, the strain of amatory raillery (or marital hostility) is voiced under the cloak of anonymity by an unknown Elizabethan poet.

> A woman's looks
> Are barbéd hooks
> That catch by art
> The strongest heart.

For the most part, however, the comedy of love consists of teasing, exchanges of badinage, a pastime which no one takes seriously. Donne mixes his physical passion with metaphysical sarcasm, but Lyly, Wither, Suckling, Congreve, and Prior are content to join fancy with facetiousness. The balance is neatly and memorably struck by Sir Walter Scott in "Marmion":

> O Woman! in our hours of ease,
> Uncertain, coy, and hard to please,
> And variable as the shade
> By the light quivering aspen made;
> When pain and anguish wring the brow,
> A ministering angel thou!

THE RECONCILIATION

Horace
How fond, how fierce, your arms to me would cling
   Before your heart made various excursions;
Then I was happier than the happiest king
     Of all the Persians.

Lydia
As long as I remained your constant flame,
   I was a proud and rather well-sung Lydia;
But now, in spite of all your precious fame,
     I'm glad I'm rid o' ye.

Horace
Ah, well, I've Chloë for my present queen;
   Her voice would thrill the marble bust of Caesar.
And I would exit gladly from the scene
     If it would please her.

You smiled, you spoke & I believed
And offer him my heart.
I was a new feeling
We saw it in each others eyes
If I should see your eyes again
Come back to me in dreams — that I
may live
Come to me in the silence of the night.
yet come to me in dreams, that I may live
With all my will, but much against my heart

Lydia
And as for me, with every burning breath,
   I think of Calaïs, my handsome lover;
For him not only would I suffer death,
      But die twice over.

Horace
What if the old love were to come once more
   With smiling face and understanding tacit,
Would you come in if I'd unbar the door?
      Or would you pass it?

Lydia
Though he's a star that's constant, strong and true,
   And you're as light as cork or wild as fever,
With all your faults I'd live and die with you,
      You old deceiver!

Horace
adapted by Louis Untermeyer

ALL SEASONS IN ONE

April is in my mistress' face,
And July in her eyes hath place,
Within her bosom is September,
But in her heart a cold December.

Anonymous

LOVE'S LIMIT

Ye bubbling springs that gentle music makes
To lovers' plaints with heart-sore throbs immixt,
Whenas my dear this way her pleasure takes,
Tell her with tears how firm my love is fixt;
And, Philomel, report my timorous fears,
And, Echo, sound my heigh-ho's in her ears.
But if she asks if I for love will die,
Tell her, Good faith, good faith, good faith—not I!

Anonymous

O STAY, SWEET LOVE

O stay, sweet love; see here the place of sporting;
  These gentle flowers smile sweetly to invite us,
And chirping birds are hitherward resorting,
  Warbling sweet notes only to delight us:
Then stay, dear love, for, tho' thou run from me,
Run ne'er so fast, yet I will follow thee.

I thought, my love, that I should overtake you;
  Sweet heart, sit down under this shadowed tree,
And I will promise never to forsake you,
  So you will grant to me a lover's fee.
Whereat she smiled, and kindly to me said,
"I never meant to live and die a maid."

Anonymous

There are countless variations of the following folk song. Several are tracked down in James Reeves' The Idiom of the People; some of the more bawdy examples can be found as early as the seventeenth century and were contained in D'Urfey's ribald Pills to Purge Melancholy. This is a coy and innocent version.

O, NO, JOHN

On yonder hill there stands a creature;
 Who she is I do not know.
I'll go ask her hand in marriage,
 And she'll answer yes or no.
"O, no, John, no, John, no, John, no."

Madam, in your face is beauty;
 On your lips red roses grow.
Will you take me for your husband?
 Madam, answer yes or no.
"O, no, John, no, John, no, John, no."

"My father was a Spanish captain,
 Went to sea a year ago.
First he kissed me, then he left me,
 Bade me always answer no.
So no, John, no, John, no, John, no."

Madam, since you are so cruel,
 And since you do scorn me so,
If I may not be your husband,
 Madam, will you let me go?
"O, no, John, no, John, no, John, no."

Hark! I hear the church-bells ringing;
 Will you come and be my wife?
Or, dear madam, have you settled
 To be single all your life?
"O, no, John, no, John, no, John, no!"

Anonymous

KISSIN'

Some say kissin's a sin,
　　But I say not at a';
For it's been in the warld
　　Ever since there were twa.

If it were na lawful,
　　Lawyers wad na 'low it;
If it were na holy,
　　Ministers wad no do it.

If it were na decent,
　　Maidens wad na let it;
If it were na plenty
　　Poor folk could na get it.

Anonymous

History remembers Sir Thomas Wyatt because of two things: he introduced the sonnet into England, and he was Anne Boleyn's lover before she was married to Henry VIII. Although his sonnet-pioneering marks a milestone in English literature, Wyatt is insufficiently appreciated for having revived the lyrical spirit in England with a blend of elevated sentiments and colloquial phrases.

Wyatt's best known poem, "The Forsaken Lover," is on page 71.

THE LOVER REJOICETH

Tangled was I in Love's snare,
Oppressed with pain, torment with care;
Of grief right sure, of joy quite bare,
Clean in despair by cruelty.
But ha! ha! ha! full well is me,
For I am now at liberty.

The woeful days so full of pain,
The weary nights all spent in vain,
The labor lost for so small gain,
To write them all it will not be.
But ha! ha! ha! full well is me,
For I am now at liberty.

With feignéd words which were but wind
To long delays was I assign'd;
Her wily looks my wits did blind;
Whate'er she would I would agree.
But ha! ha! ha! full well is me,
For I am now at liberty.

Was never bird tangled in lime
That broke away in better time,
Than I, that rotten boughs did climb
And had no hurt but 'scapéd free.
Now ha! ha! ha! full well is me,
For I am now at liberty.

Sir Thomas Wyatt

ADVICE TO A GIRL

Never love unless you can
Bear with all the faults of man!
Men sometimes will jealous be,
Though but little cause they see,
And hang the head as discontent,
And speak what straight they will repent.

Men that but one saint adore,
Make a show of love to more;
Beauty must be scorned in none,
Though but truly served in one:
For what is courtship but disguise?
True hearts may have dissembling eyes.

Men, when their affairs require,
Must awhile themselves retire;
Sometimes hunt, and sometimes hawk,
And not ever sit and talk—
If these and such—like you can bear,
Then like, and love, and never fear!

Thomas Campion

GOOD ADVICE

Ladies, fly from Love's smooth tale!
Oaths steeped in tears so oft prevail;
Grief is infectious, and the air
Inflamed with sighs will blast the fair!
Then stop your ears when lovers cry
Lest yourself weep, when no soft eye
Shall with a sorrowing tear repay
That pity which you cast away.

Young men, fly when Beauty darts
Amorous glances at your hearts!
The fixed mark gives the shooter aim
And ladies' looks have power to maim;
Now 'twixt their lips, now in their eyes,
Wrapped in a smile, or kiss, Love lies.
Then fly betimes, for only they
Conquer Love that run away!

Thomas Carew

SIGH NO MORE

Sigh no more, ladies, sigh no more;
  Men were deceivers ever;
One foot in sea, and one on shore,
  To one thing constant never:
Then sigh not so, but let them go,
  And be you blithe and bonny,
Converting all your sounds of woe
  Into "Hey nonny, nonny!"

Sing no more ditties, sing no moe,
  Of dumps so dull and heavy;
The fraud of men was ever so,
  Since summer first was leavy:
Then sigh not so, but let them go,
  And be you blithe and bonny,
Converting all your sounds of woe
  Into "Hey nonny, nonny!"

William Shakespeare

The dramas of the sixteenth-century John Lyly are completely forgotten, but his prose romance, Euphues, gave us a word suggesting a style which set a fashion until it was ridiculed (by Shakespeare, among others) to death. Euphuisms are characterized by highly affected phrases, artificial figures of speech, far-fetched allusions, and elaborate antitheses which make little sense. There were, however, times when Lyly was direct, witty, and far from euphuistic, as in the following piece of badinage.

CARDS FOR KISSES

Cupid and my Campaspe played
At cards for kisses; Cupid paid:
He stakes his quiver, bow and arrows,
His mother's doves, and team of sparrows;
Loses them too; then down he throws
The coral of his lip, the rose
Growing on's cheek (but none knows how);
With these, the crystal of his brow,
And then the dimple of his chin.
All these did my Campaspe win.
At last he set her both his eyes.
She won, and Cupid blind did rise.
O Love! has she done this to thee?
What shall, alas! become of me?

John Lyly

BELINDA THE CHARITABLE

Belinda has such wond'rous charms,
'Tis heaven to lie within her arms;
And she's so charitably given,
She wishes all mankind in heaven.

Anonymous

Greatest of the metaphysical poets, John Donne led a lifelong struggle between flesh and the spirit. The struggle was synthesized in a kind of agonized wit. He indulged in paradox; he was not above puns. When his clandestine marriage to the sixteen-year-old Anne More resulted in his arrest and imprisonment, he summed up the situation in a short sentence: "John Donne—Anne Donne—Undone."

"Song: Catch a Falling Star" is a poem in which amusement and cynicism are joined. A more impassioned lyric, "Sweetest Love, I Do Not Go," is on page 76.

SONG: CATCH A FALLING STAR

Go and catch a falling star,
    Get with child a mandrake root,
Tell me where all past years are,
    Or who cleft the Devil's foot;
Teach me to hear mermaids singing,

Or to keep off envy's stinging,
     And find
     What wind
Serves to advance an honest mind.

If thou be'st born to strange sights,
    Things invisible to see,
Ride ten thousand days and nights
    Till Age snow white hairs on thee;
Thou, when thou return'st, wilt tell me
All strange wonders that befell thee,
     And swear
     No where
Lives a woman true and fair.

If thou find'st one, let me know;
    Such a pilgrimage were sweet.
Yet do not; I would not go,
    Though at next door we might meet.
Though she were true when you met her,
And last till you write your letter,
     Yet she
     Will be
False, ere I come, to two or three.

John Donne

Seventeenth-century George Wither was another poet who did not despise punning. He had this couplet inscribed beneath his portrait:

I Grow and Wither
Both together.

Although he wrote a satire entitled "Abuses Stripped and Whipped" which was so bitter that he was sent to prison, Wither was at his best in lighter persiflage like "The Theft" and "What Care I."

THE THEFT

Now gentle sleep hath closéd up those eyes
Which, waking, kept my boldest thoughts in awe;
And free access unto that sweet lip lies
From whence I long the rosy breath to draw.
Methinks no wrong it were if I should steal
From those two melting rubies one poor kiss;
None sees the theft that would the theft reveal,
Nor rob I her of aught that she can miss.

Nay, should I twenty kisses take away,
There would be little sign I would do so.
Why then should I this robbery delay?
Oh, she may wake, and therewith angry grow?
Well, if she do, I'll back restore that one,
And twenty hundred thousand more for loan!

George Wither

WHAT CARE I

Shall I, wasting in despair,
Die because a woman's fair?
Or my cheeks make pale with care
'Cause another's rosy are?
Be she fairer than the day
Or the flowery meads in May—
 If she be not so to me,
 What care I how fair she be?

Shall my foolish heart be pined
'Cause I see a woman kind?
Or a well disposéd nature
Joinéd with a lovely feature?
Be she meeker, kinder, than
Turtle-dove or pelican,
    If she be not so to me,
    What care I how kind she be?

Shall a woman's virtues move
Me to perish for her love?
Or her merits' value known
Make me quite forget mine own?
Be she with that goodness blest
Which may gain her name of Best;
    If she seem not such to me,
    What care I how good she be?

'Cause her fortune seems too high,
Shall I play the fool and die?
Those that bear a noble mind
Where they want of riches find,
Think what with them they would do
Who without them dare to woo;
    And unless that mind I see,
    What care I how great she be?

Great or good, or kind or fair,
I will ne'er the more despair;
If she love me, this believe,
I will die ere she shall grieve;
If she slight me when I woo,
I can scorn and let her go.
    For if she be not for me,
    What care I for whom she be?

George Wither

THE TOUCHSTONE

A fool and a knave with different views
    For Julia's hand apply;
The knave to mend his fortune sues,
    The fool to please his eye.

Ask you how Julia will behave?
    Depend on't for a rule.
If she's a fool, she'll wed the knave;
    If she's a knave, the fool.

Samuel Bishop

UNDER THE WILLOW-SHADES

Under the willow-shades they were
    Free from the eye-sight of the sun,
For no intruding beam could there
    Peep through to spy what things were done:
        Thus sheltered they unseen did lie,
        Surfeiting on each other's eye;
Defended by the willow-shades alone,
The sun's heat they defied and cooled their own.

Whilst they did embrace unspied,
    The conscious willow seemed to smile,
That them with privacy supplied,
    Holding the door, as 't were, the while;
        And when their dalliances were o'er,
        The willows, to oblige them more,
Bowing, did seem to say, as they withdrew,
"We can supply you with a cradle too."

William Davenant

THAT FOND IMPOSSIBILITY

Why shouldst thou swear I am forsworn,
    Since thine I vowed to be?
Lady, it is already morn,
    And 'twas last night I swore to thee
    That fond impossibility.

Have I not loved thee much and long,
    A tedious twelve hours' space?
I should all other beauties wrong,
    And rob thee of a new embrace
    Should I still dote upon thy face.

Not but all joy in thy brown hair
  In others may be found;
But I must search the black and fair,
  Like skilful mineralists that sound
  For treasure in un-plowed-up ground.

Then if, when I have loved my round,
  Thou prov'st the pleasant she,
With spoils of meaner beauties crowned
  I laden will return to thee,
  Even sated with variety.

Richard Lovelace

THE CONSTANT LOVER

Out upon it, I have loved
  Three whole days together!
And am like to love three more
  If it prove fair weather.

Time shall moult away his wings
  Ere he shall discover
In the whole wide world again
  Such a constant lover.

But the spite on't is, no praise
  Is due at all to me:
Love with me had made no stays
  Had it any been but she.

Had it any been but she,
  And that very face,
There had been at least ere this
  A dozen in her place.

Sir John Suckling

43

WHY SO PALE AND WAN?

Why so pale and wan, fond lover?
  Prithee, why so pale?
Will, when looking well can't move her,
  Looking ill prevail?
  Prithee, why so pale?

Why so dull and mute, young sinner?
  Prithee, why so mute?
Will, when speaking well can't win her,
  Saying nothing do 't?
  Prithee, why so mute?

Quit, quit for shame! This will not move;
  This cannot take her.
If of herself she will not love,
  Nothing can make her.
  The devil take her!

Sir John Suckling

SWEET, LET ME GO

Sweet, let me go! sweet, let me go!
What do you mean to vex me so?
Cease your pleading force!
Do you think thus to extort remorse?
Now, now! no more! alas, you over bear me,
And I would cry—but some, I fear, might hear me.

William Corkine

Aphra Behn was a most extraordinary woman. Daughter of a seventeenth-century barber, she was, among many other things, the first English professional authoress. She spent her childhood in Surinam, and, after her return to England, married a Dutch merchant. A widow at twenty-six, she became a professional spy, lived extravagantly in Antwerp, and, back in London, was imprisoned for debt. She then began to write poems, pamphlets, and plays in the loose, libidinous Restoration manner. Before she was forty she had written fifteen dramas, countless verses, and several novels, one of which, Oroonoko, anticipated Rousseau's conception of the "noble savage." She flaunted her way in and out of society and, in spite of scandal, was buried in Westminster Abbey.

"AND FORGIVE US OUR TRESPASSES"

How prone we are to sin; how sweet were made
The pleasures our resistless hearts invade.
Of all my crimes, the breach of all thy laws,
Love, soft bewitching love, has been the cause.
Of all the paths that vanity has trod,
That sure will soonest be forgiven by God.
If things on earth may be to heaven resembled,
It must be love, pure, constant, undissembled.
But if to sin by chance the charmer press,
Forgive, O Lord, forgive our trespasses.

Aphra Behn

MAN IS FOR THE WOMAN MADE

Man is for the woman made
And the woman made for man.
As the spur is for the jade,
As the scabbard for the blade,
As for digging is the spade,
   As for liquor is the can,
So man is for the woman made,
   And the woman made for, man.

As the sceptre's to be swayed,
As for night's the serenade,
   As for pudding is the pan,
   And to cool us is the fan,
So man is for the woman made,
   And the woman made for man.

Be she widow, wife, or maid,
Be she wanton, be she staid,
Be she well or ill arrayed,
   Slut or shrew or harridan,
Yet man is for the woman made,
   And the woman made for man.

   Peter Anthony Motteaux

The eighteenth-century poets and playwrights seldom took lovers seriously. To them, love was a provocative if not always pleasurable game; if their poetry was formal and artificial, we must remember that formal verse was the proper expression of the period and that artifice was considered a kind of art.

John Dryden epitomized his epoch. He despised the taste of his day, but he catered to it. There was nothing he could not do. He was equally adroit in translations from the classics and piquant versifying, such as the example which follows.

FALSE AND FICKLE

Fair Iris I love, and hourly I die,
But not for a lip nor a languishing eye.
She's fickle and false, and there we agree,
For I am as false and as fickle as she.
We neither believe what either can say,
And, neither believing, we neither betray.

'Tis civil to swear and say things, of course;
We mean not the taking for better for worse.
When present we love, when absent, agree;
I think not of Iris, nor Iris of me.
The legend of love no couple can find
So easy to part, or so equally joined.

John Dryden

Lady Mary Wortley Montagu was one of the eighteenth century's great belles. Famous as a beauty, she was also a wit, a brilliant letter-writer and, from time to time, a poet. A friend of Pope, she quarreled with him, became his enemy, and replied to his attack with a furious defense. Suddenly, without warning and without explanation, she left her husband and her country, lived abroad, and died, a stubborn eccentric, in her seventies.

RESTRAINED PASSION

Dear Colin, prevent my warm blushes,
Since how can I speak without pain?
My eyes have oft told you my wishes,
Oh can't you their meaning explain?

My passion would lose by expression,
    And you too might cruelly blame;
Then don't you expect a confession
    Of what is too tender to name.

Since yours is the province of speaking,
    Why should you expect it from me?
Our wishes should be in our keeping,
    Till you tell us what they should be:
Then quickly why don't you discover,
    Did your heart feel such tortures as mine;
I need not tell over and over
    What I in my bosom confine.

Lady Mary Wortley Montagu

Author of several vivacious comedies which are occasionally revived, William Congreve is continually quoted by thousands who never heard of him. It was Congreve, not (as some suppose) Shakespeare, who wrote "Music has charms to soothe the savage breast," and it was Congreve who made his characters give us such usable phrases as "She lays it on with a trowel," "murder will out," "kiss and tell," "the way of all flesh," "Hell has no fury like a woman scorned."

FALSE THOUGH SHE BE

False though she be to me and love,
    I'll never seek revenge;
For still the charmer I approve,
    Though I deplore her change.

In hours of bliss we oft have met;
    They could not always last.
And though the present I regret,
    I'm grateful for the past.

William Congreve

ALL OR NOTHING

Fair Selinda goes to prayers
    If I but ask the favor;
And yet the tender fool's in tears
    When she believes I'll leave her.

Would I were free from this restraint,
  Or else had hopes to win her.
Would she could make of me a saint,
  Or I of her a sinner!

                              William Congreve

The eighteenth-century Matthew Prior started out as a classical scholar—at thirteen he translated Latin poetry into English—but he became famous as a writer who teased a frivolous society. His verses were so sly and his lines so neatly turned that his lapses were forgiven— including the bad grammar in the last stanza of the following poem . . . For the reference to Horace and Lydia, also in the last stanza, see "The Reconciliation" on page 30.

ANSWER TO JEALOUSY

Dear Chloe, how blubbered is that pretty face;
  Thy cheek all on fire, thy hair all uncurled:
Prythee quit this caprice, and (as old Falstaff says)
  Let us e'en talk a little like folks of this world.

How canst thou presume, thou hast leave to destroy
  The beauties which Venus but lent to thy keeping?
Those looks were designed to inspire love and joy:
  More ord'nary eyes may serve people for weeping.

To be vexed at a trifle or two that I writ,
  Your judgment at once and my passion you wrong:
You take that for fact, which will scarce be found wit.
  Odds life! must one swear to the truth of a song?

What I speak, my fair Chloe, and what I write, shows
  The difference there is betwixt nature and art.
I court others in verse; but I love thee in prose:
  And they have my whimsies, but thou hast my heart.

The god of us verse-men (you know, child) the Sun,
  How after his journeys he sets up his rest:
If at morning o'er earth 'tis his fancy to run,
  At night he declines on his Thetis's breast.

So when I am wearied with wandering all day,
   To thee, my delight, in the evening I come:
No matter what beauties I saw in my way,
   They were all but my visits, but thou art my home.

Then finish, dear Chloe, this pastoral war;
   And let us, like Horace and Lydia, agree:
For thou art a girl as much brighter than her,
   As he was a poet sublimer than me.

Matthew Prior

THE ANGRY LOVER

As Chloe came into the room t'other day,
I peevish began: "Where so long did you stay?
In your lifetime you never regarded the hour.
You promised at two, and (pray look, child) 'tis four!
A lady's watch needs neither figures nor wheels—
'Tis enough that 'tis loaded with baubles and seals.
A temper so heedless no mortal can bear—"
Thus far I went on with a resolute air.
"Lord bless me," said she, "let a body but speak!
Here's an ugly, hard rosebud fall'n onto my neck.
It has hurt me and vexed me to such a degree—
See here—for you never believe me—pray see,
On the side of my breast, what a mark it has made!"
So saying, her bosom she careless displayed.
That seat of delight I with wonder surveyed—
And forgot every word I designed to have said.

Matthew Prior

A TRUE MAID

"No! No! For my virginity,
When I lose that," said Rose, "I'll die!"
"Behind the elms last night," said Dick,
"Rose, were you not extremely sick?"

Matthew Prior

SONG: THE DISSEMBLER

The merchant, to secure his treasure,
  Conveys it in a borrowed name:
Euphelia serves to grace my measure,
  But Chloe is my real flame.

My softest verse, my darling lyre
  Upon Euphelia's toilet lay—
When Chloe noted her desire
  That I should sing, that I should play.

My lyre I tune, my voice I raise,
  But with my numbers mix my sighs;
And whilst I sing Euphelia's praise,
  I fix my soul on Chloe's eyes.

Fair Chloe blushed; Euphelia frowned:
  I sung, and gazed; I played, and trembled:
And Venus to the Loves around
  Remarked how ill we all dissembled.

Matthew Prior

A REASONABLE AFFLICTION

The laughter of love

On his death-bed poor Lubin lies:
   His spouse is in despair;
With frequent cries, and mutual sighs,
   They both express their care.

"A different cause," says Parson Sly,
   "The same effect may give:
Poor Lubin fears that he may die;
   His wife, that he may live."

Matthew Prior

One of the most popular men of his time, Thomas Moore knew
everyone worth knowing and wrote on everything worth reading. His
Irish Melodies made him Ireland's national songwriter; his translations
of Anacreon were considered the most fluent (if also the most facile)
ever attempted; his Lalla Rookh was hailed as a resplendent retelling of
Oriental tales in verse; his Life of Byron started an exciting controversy;
his posthumously published writings ran to eight volumes. First and
last a natural singer (vocal as well as verbal), Moore charmed with light
lyrics in the style of "The Time I've Lost in Wooing."

THE TIME I'VE LOST IN WOOING

The time I've lost in wooing,
In watching and pursuing
   The light that lies
   In woman's eyes,
Has been my heart's undoing.
Though Wisdom oft has sought me,
I scorned the lore she brought me,
   My only books
   Were woman's looks,
And folly's all they've taught me.

Her smile when Beauty granted,
I hung with gaze enchanted,
Like him the Sprite,
   Whom maids by night
Oft meet in glen that's haunted.

51

Like him, too, Beauty won me,
But while her eyes were on me,
  If once their ray
  Was turned away,
O, winds could not outrun me.

And are those follies going?
And is my proud heart growing
  Too cold or wise
  For brilliant eyes
Again to set it glowing?
No; vain, alas! th' endeavor
From bonds so sweet to sever—
  Poor Wisdom's chance
  Against a glance
Is now as weak as ever.

Thomas Moore

Creator of such major performances as "The Rime of the Ancient
Mariner" and "Kubla Khan," the fitful Samuel Taylor Coleridge some-
times took pleasure in trivia. The following, adapted from the German
of Gotthold Lessing, is one of his trifles.

BY WHAT SWEET NAME

I asked my fair, one happy day,
What I should call her in my lay;
  By what sweet name from Rome or Greece.
Lalage, Neæra, Chloris,
Sappho, Lesbia, or Doris,
  Arethusa or Lucrece.

"Ah," replied my gentle fair,
"Belovéd, what are names but air?
  Choose whatever suits the line.
Call me Sappho, call me Chloris,
Call me Lalage or Doris,
  Only—only call me thine!"

Samuel Taylor Coleridge

Browning was in a light mood when he wrote "Adam, Lilith, and Eve," a poem in a series he called Jocoseria. It presents a modern and rather odd situation: a man (Adam), the woman he might have married (Lilith), and the woman he did marry (Eve). A storm frightens the women and they confess· their feelings about Adam in the past. When the storm is over they treat the whole thing as a joke.

ADAM, LILITH, AND EVE

One day, it thundered and lightened.
Two women, fairly frightened,
Sank to their knees, transformed, transfixed,
At the feet of the man who sat betwixt;
And "Mercy!" cried each—"if I tell the truth
Of a passage in my youth!"

Said This: "Do you mind the morning
I met your love with scorning?
As the worst of the venom left my lips,
I thought, 'If, despite this lie, he strips
The mask from my soul with a kiss—I crawl
His slave,—soul, body, and all!'"

Said That: "We stood to be married;
The priest, or some one, tarried;
'If Paradise-door prove locked?' smiled you.
I thought, as I nodded, smiling too,
'Did one, that's away, arrive—nor late
Nor soon should unlock Hell's gate!'"

It ceased to lighten and thunder.
Up started both in wonder,
Looked round and saw that the sky was clear,
Then laughed "Confess you believed us, Dear!"
"I saw through the joke!" the man replied
They re-seated themselves beside.

Robert Browning

53

WHENEVER WE HAPPEN TO KISS

She shuts her eyes and keeps them shut
  Whenever we happen to kiss.
I smile at her behavior, but
  Ask what she means by this.

Day after day, night after night,
  I question why it is
She shuts her eyes and holds them tight
  Whenever we happen to kiss.

Is it decorum or delight
  When, at the moment of bliss,
She shuts her eyes and holds them tight
  Whenever we happen to kiss?

Heinrich Heine
adapted by Louis Untermeyer

SUSPICIOUS SWEETHEART

"Why those deep sighs?" I ask her.
  "You tremble when we touch.
Here we are close together.
  What troubles you so much?"

"Can you not hear my heart beat?
  It echoes through the room."
She nods her head and murmurs,
  "It beats—God knows for whom."

Heinrich Heine
adapted by Louis Untermeyer

THE KISS

"I saw him kiss your cheek!"—"'Tis true."
"O Modesty!"—"'Twas strictly kept:
He thought me asleep; at least, I knew
He thought I thought he thought I slept."

Coventry Patmore

The poetry of A. E. Housman is distinguished not only by its pared precision but also by its contradictions. It is forthright yet fastidious, sentimental yet satirical, lyrical yet humorous—and the humor is both pungent and poignant. A combination of balladlike simplicity and understated irony intensifies the three following poems from A Shropshire Lad.

WHEN I WAS ONE-AND-TWENTY

When I was one-and-twenty
  I heard a wise man say,
"Give crowns and pounds and guineas
  But not your heart away;
Give pearls away and rubies
  But keep your fancy free."
But I was one-and-twenty,
  No use to talk to me.

When I was one-and-twenty
  I heard him say again,
"The heart out of the bosom
  Was never given in vain;
'Tis paid with sighs a plenty
  And sold for endless rue."
And I am two-and-twenty,
  And oh, 'tis true, 'tis true.

A. E. *Housman*

OH, WHEN I WAS IN LOVE WITH YOU

Oh, when I was in love with you,
  Then I was clean and brave,
And miles around the wonder grew
  How well did I behave.

And now the fancy passes by,
  And nothing will remain,
And miles around they'll say that I
  Am quite myself again.

A. E. *Housman*

The following poem may have been suggested by Shakespeare's "In the Spring-Time" (see page 4). But Housman makes the spring-time wooing take another and more comic turn. It is a frustrated love lyric that is also a burlesque ballad.

OH, SEE HOW THICK THE GOLDCUP FLOWERS

Oh, see how thick the goldcup flowers
    Are lying in field and lane,
With dandelions to tell the hours
    That never are told again.
Oh, may I squire you round the meads
    And pick you posies gay?
—'Twill do no harm to take my arm.
    "You may, young man, you may."

Ah, spring was sent for lass and lad,
    'Tis now the blood runs gold,
And man and maid had best be glad
    Before the world is old.
What flowers to-day may flower to-morrow,
    But never as good as new.
—Suppose I wound my arm right round—
    " 'Tis true, young man, 'tis true."

Some lads there are, 'tis shame to say,
    That only court to thieve,
And once they bear the bloom away
    'Tis little enough they leave.
Then keep your heart for men like me
    And safe from trustless chaps.
My love is true and all for you.
    "Perhaps, young man, perhaps."

Oh, look in my eyes then, can you doubt?
    Why! 'tis a mile from town!
How green the grass is all about!
    We might as well sit down.
—Ah, life what is it but a flower?
    Why must true lovers sigh?
Be kind, have pity, my own, my pretty—
    "Good-bye, young man, good-bye."

A. E. Housman

Born in the same year (1884) two poets—an American, Sara Teasdale, and an Englishwoman, Anna Wickham—gave an old theme new variations. The conventional sentimentalities were subjected to sly, sidelong thrusts.

Two other, more passionate, poems by Anna Wickham are on pages 25 and 142.

NIGHT SONG AT AMALFI

I asked the heaven of stars
    What I should give my love—
It answered me with silence,
    Silence above.

I asked the darkened sea
    Down where the fishermen go—
It answered me with silence,
    Silence below.

Oh, I could give him weeping,
    Or I could give him song—
But how can I give silence
    My whole life long?

Sara Teasdale

THE TIRED MAN

I am a quiet gentleman,
And I would sit and dream;
But my wife is on the hillside
Wild as a wild hill-stream.

I am a quiet gentleman,
And I would sit and think;
But my wife is walking the whirlwind
Through a night as black as ink.

O, give me a woman of my race
As well controlled as I,
And let us sit by the fireside,
Patient until we die!

Anna Wickham

MEDITATION AT KEW

Alas! for all the pretty women who marry dull men,
Go into the suburbs and never come out again,
Who lose their pretty faces, and dim their pretty eyes,
Because no one has skill or courage to organize.

What do these pretty women suffer when they marry?
They bear a boy who is like Uncle Harry,
A girl, who is like Aunt Eliza, and not new,
These old, dull races must breed true.

I would enclose a common in the sun,
And let the young wives out to laugh and run;
I would steal their dull clothes and go away,
And leave the pretty naked things to play.

Then I would make a contract with hard Fate
That they see all the men in the world and choose a mate,
And I would summon all the pipers in the town
That they dance with Love at a feast, and dance him down.

From the gay unions of choice
We'd have a race of splendid beauty, and of thrilling voice.
The World whips frank, gay love with rods,
But frankly, gayly shall we get the gods.

Anna Wickham

EQUALS

You child, how can you dare complain
    That you and I may be mismated
Because, you say, you lack a brain
    And I'm so highly educated.

The body is the greater thing;
    And you are greatly gifted when
You have such hands and breasts that bring
    More peace than all the words of men.

Take pride in this, your beauty; drink
    The wine it offers for our love.
Be glad you do not have to think;
    One thoughtful lover is enough.

We're equal partners, that is plain.
    Our life cannot grow dull or shoddy,
While I have such a lovely brain,
    And you have such a lively body.

Louis Untermeyer

Merrill Moore was a practicing psychiatrist who was also the most facile of poets. It was estimated that he had composed close to forty thousand sonnets before he died at fifty-four. He turned the smallest incidents as well as his patients' case histories into vivid fourteen-line poems—one of his many volumes, appropriately entitled M, contained one thousand fresh, free-rhyming, and seemingly impromptu "American" sonnets. He gave the traditional tight form a surprising flexibility and a new conversational tone.

HOW SHE RESOLVED TO ACT

"I shall be careful to say nothing at all
About myself, or what I know of him,
Or the vaguest thought I have, no matter how dim,
Tonight, if it so happen that he call."
And not ten minutes later the door-bell rang,
And into the hall he stepped as he always did,
With a face and a bearing that quite poorly hid
His brain that burned, and his heart that fairly sang,
And his tongue that wanted to be rid of the truth.

As well as she could, for she was very loath
To signify how she felt, she kept very still.
But soon her heart cracked loud as a coffee-mill,
And her brain swung like a comet in the dark,
And her tongue raced like a squirrel in the park.

Merrill Moore

Besides being a poet, Clinch Calkins (Marion Merrell) was a social worker and a novelist who caught the temper of her times. Her poetry is marked by a delicate whimsy and—as manifest in the internal rhymes of "Mourning Dove"—fastidious craftsmanship.

MOURNING DOVE

The seemingly lovely mourning dove is but a churl,
Cross to his mate. She, crossed like any girl,
Does not accept his malice lightly. But malice is unsightly
In two supposed to be in love. So, for the spectator,
He must not seem to hate her. They gently pair away
In park-like walk, acknowledging here and there
A friendly stare;
So everyone can say of them in envy, what is more romantic
In a frantic world, what is more adorning,
Seen against its bellicose mechanics,
Than the lovely mourning dove?

Clinch Calkins

Ogden Nash has a wayward way with rhymes. Only he could write a two-line ode to a baby:

A bit of talcum
Is always walcum.

Only he could combine banter about breakfast foods with so unexpected and yet logical a pun as:

Our daily diet grows odder and odder—
It's a wise child that knows its fodder.

The following poem has its quota of stretch-rhymes ("anything-Vienna thing," "Thackeray's-Daiquiris," for example) but it is the singular reason that makes the rhymes inevitable.

THAT REMINDS ME

Just imagine yourself seated on a shadowy terrace,
And beside you is a girl who stirs you more strangely than an heiress.
It is a summer evening at its most superb,
And the moonlight reminds you that To Love is an active verb,
And the stars are twinkling like anything,
And a distant orchestra is playing some sentimental old Vienna thing,
And your hand clasps hers, which rests there without shrinking,
And after a silence fraught with romance you ask her what she is
    thinking,
And she starts and returns from the moon-washed distances to the
    shadowy veranda,
And says, Oh, I was wondering how many bamboo shoots a day it
    takes to feed a baby Giant Panda.
Or you stand with her on a hilltop and gaze on a winter sunset,
And everything is as starkly beautiful as a page from Sigrid Undset,
And your arm goes round her waist and you make an avowal which
    for masterfully marshaled emotional content might have been a
    page of Ouida's or Thackeray's,
And after a silence fraught with romance she says, I forgot to order
    the limes for the Daiquiris.
Or in a twilight drawing room you have just asked the most momen-
    tous of questions,
And after a silence fraught with romance she says I think this little
    table would look better where that little table is, but then where
    would that little table go, have you any suggestions?
And that's the way they go around hitting below our belts;
It isn't that nothing is sacred to them, it's just that at the Sacred
    Moment they are always thinking of something else.

Ogden Nash

*John Betjeman had published more than a dozen volumes without
causing any excitement until Slick but Not Streamlined appeared in
1947. It contained an introduction by W. H. Auden which began:
"It is difficult to write judiciously about a poet whose work makes
one violently jealous." Ten years later Betjeman's Collected Poems
became a sensational success in England. Winning award after award,
it appealed to readers of every class because its mixture of wistful
sentiment and quiet wit was straightforward, unaffected, and English
to the core.*

A SUBALTERN'S LOVE-SONG

Miss J. Hunter Dunn, Miss J. Hunter Dunn,
Furnish'd and burnish'd by Aldershot sun,
What strenuous singles we played after tea,
We in the tournament—you against me!

Love-thirty, love-forty, oh! weakness of joy,
The speed of a swallow, the grace of a boy,
With carefullest carelessness, gaily you won,
I am weak from your loveliness, Joan Hunter Dunn.

Miss Joan Hunter Dunn, Miss Joan Hunter Dunn,
How mad I am, sad I am, glad that you won.
The warm-handled racket is back in its press,
But my shock-headed victor, she loves me no less.

Her father's euonymus shines as we walk,
And swing past the summer-house, buried in talk,
And cool the verandah that welcomes us in
To the six-o'clock news and a lime-juice and gin.

The scent of the conifers, sound of the bath,
The view from my bedroom of moss-dappled path,
As I struggle with double-end evening tie,
For we dance at the Golf Club, my victor and I.

On the floor of her bedroom lie blazer and shorts
And the cream-coloured walls are be-trophied with sports,
And westering, questioning settles the sun
On your low-leaded window, Miss Joan Hunter Dunn.

The Hillman is waiting, the light's in the hall,
The pictures of Egypt are bright on the wall.
My sweet, I am standing beside the oak stair,
And there on the landing's the light on your hair.

By roads "not adopted", by woodlanded ways,
She drove to the club in the late summer haze,
Into nine-o'clock Camberley, heavy with bells
And mushroomy, pine-woody, evergreen smells.

Miss Joan Hunter Dunn, Miss Joan Hunter Dunn,
I can hear from the car-park the dance has begun.
Oh! full Surrey twilight! importunate band!
Oh! strongly adorable tennis-girl's hand!

Around us are Rovers and Austins afar;
Above us, the intimate roof of the car;
And here on my right is the girl of my choice,
With the tilt of her nose and the chime of her voice,

And the scent of her wrap, and the words never said,
And the ominous, ominous dancing ahead.
We sat in the car park till twenty to one,
And now I'm engaged to Miss Joan Hunter Dunn.

John Betjeman

Judith Viorst's idiom is as American as Betjeman's is English. The manner is established in the titles of her books, The Village Square— the Greenwich Village pun is significant—and It's Hard to Be Hip Over Thirty, and Other Tragedies of Married Life. The "tragedies" are those of a modern young woman who had looked forward to orgies and bouts of illicit passion but found herself surrounded by automatic dishwashers, garbage disposal units, and countless cans of strained baby food.

TRUE LOVE

It is true love because
I put on eyeliner and a concerto and make pungent observations about
    the great issues of the day
Even when there's no one here but him,
And because
I do not resent watching the Green Bay Packers
Even though I am philosophically opposed to football,
And because
When he is late for dinner and I know he must be either having an
    affair or lying dead in the middle of the street,
I always hope he's dead.

It's true love because
If he said quit drinking martinis but I kept drinking them and the
    next morning I couldn't get out of bed,
He wouldn't tell me he told me,
And because
He is willing to wear unironed undershorts
Out of respect for the fact that I am philosophically opposed to ironing,
And because
If his mother was drowning and I was drowning and he had to choose
    one of us to save,
He says he'd save me.

It's true love because
When he went to San Francisco on business while I had to stay home
    with the painters and the exterminator and the baby who was
    getting the chicken pox,
He understood why I hated him,
And because
When I said that playing the stock market was juvenile and irresponsible
    and then the stock I wouldn't let him buy went up twenty-six points,
I understood why he hated me,
And because
Despite cigarette cough, tooth decay, acid indigestion, dandruff, and
    other features of married life that tend to dampen the fires of
    passion,
We still feel something
We can call
True love.

Judith Viorst

CAPSULE CONCLUSIONS

Since fret and care are everywhere,
    Give freely, lass; live fully, lover;
For death's a rather long affair,
    And when we die, we die all over.

The man who shuns Wine, Woman, and Song
Remains a fool his whole life long.

Love's a misery, there's no question,
Almost as bad as indigestion.

Listen, lass, if you would be
    Safe from every sort of scourge in
This lifelong uncertainty,
    Remain a virgin.

A comfort and a true companion
    Whose tongue with gall and honey drips,
Woman is like a kitchen onion
    That makes us weep—and smack our lips.

    Sparrows need
    To feed on seed;
Bees must have their clover;
    Girls believe
    And men deceive
The whole world over.

The foolish man who boasts that he is able
    To manage a horse or a woman without a bit,
Will never coax a mare to stay in his stable,
    And as for his bed—he'll sleep alone in it.

Lovers who please each other,
Tease each other.

Away from love and marriage, hurry!
    Run while you can from your desire!
The cooked goose has no time to worry
    Whether it's frying pan or fire.

Old German Proverbs
adapted by Louis Untermeyer

The
Pain
of
Love

Hailing the end of winter and the coming of Spring, Rupert Brooke brought what might have been a happy "Song" to this conclusion:

> The hawthorn hedge puts forth its buds,
> And my heart puts forth its pain.

Pain is as much a part of love as passion. Gladness is often mixed with grief; frustration is as common in love as fulfillment. In "The Forsaken Lover" the sixteenth-century Sir Thomas Wyatt mournfully complained of the infidelity of his sweetheart; Sir Philip Sidney echoed the grievance in "With how sad steps, O Moon"; Michael Drayton began a sonnet grimly: "Since there's no help, come, let us kiss and part."

Many of the most memorable love poems are composed around the theme of parting and pain. The double strain is united in Ovid's amorous agonizing, in the physical-metaphysical protestation of Donne's "Sweetest love, I do not go/ For weariness of thee," in Keats' agonized appeal "I cry your mercy—pity—love—aye, love," in Byron's muted "When we two parted," and in the heartbroken lyrics of Christina Rossetti and Emily Dickinson.

Here are the fears and the anguished farewells, the torments that seem to have a thousand knives. Here the heart struggles and, in its very suffering, achieves a catharsis, an alleviation and a triumph over pain.

Publius Ovidius Naso, commonly known as Ovid, wrote more poems than any other Roman poet, poems that are vivid, full of gusto, and almost exclusively concerned with love. His most famous works are Loves, The Art of Love, and the romantic-mythological Metamorphoses, a series of love poems on the changing forms of passion. The translations from Ovid's Amores (Loves) which follow are by the Elizabethan poet-dramatist, Christopher Marlowe.

Long have I borne much, mad thy faults me make;
Dishonest love, my wearied breast forsake!
Now have I freed myself, and fled the chain,
And what I have borne, shame to bear again.
We vanquish, and tread tamed love under feet,
Victorious wreaths at length my temples greet.
Suffer, and harden: good grows by this grief,
Oft bitter juice brings to the sick relief.
I have sustained, so oft thrust from the door,
To lay my body on the hard moist floor.
I know not whom thou lewdly didst embrace,
When I to watch supplied a servant's place.
I saw went forth a tired lover went,
His side past service, and his courage spent,
Yet this is less than if he had seen me;
May that shame fall mine enemies' chance to be.
When have not I, fixed to thy side, close laid?
I have thy husband, guard, and fellow played.
The people by my company she pleased;
My love was cause that more men's love she seized.
What, should I tell her vain tongue's filthy lies,
And, to my loss, god-wronging perjuries?
What secret becks in banquets with her youths,
With privy signs, and talk dissembling truths?
Hearing her to be sick, I thither ran,
But with my rival sick she was not than.
These hardened me, with what I keep obscure:
Some other seek, who will these things endure.
Now my ship in the wished haven crowned,
With joy hears Neptune's swelling waters sound.
Leave thy once-powerful words, and flatteries,
I am not as I was before, unwise.
Now love and hate my light breast each way move,
But victory, I think, will hap to love.
I'll hate, if I can; if not, love 'gainst my will,
Bulls hate the yoke, yet what they hate have still.
I fly her lust, but follow beauty's creature,
I loathe her manners, love her body's feature.
Nor with thee, nor without thee can I live,
And doubt to which desire the palm to give.
Or less fair, or less lewd would thou might'st be:

Beauty with lewdness doth right ill agree.
Her deeds gain hate, her face entreateth love;
Ah, she doth more worth than her vices prove!
Spare me, oh, by our fellow bed, by all
The gods, who by thee, to be perjured fall.
And by thy face to me a power divine,
And by thine eyes, whose radiance burns out mine!
Whate'er thou art, mine art thou: choose this course:
Wilt have me willing, or to love by force?
Rather I'll hoist up sail, and use the wind,
That I may love yet, though against my mind.

Ovid
translated by Christopher Marlowe

IN LOVE WITH TWO

Græcinus (well I wot) thou told'st me once,
I could not be in love with two at once;
By thee deceived, by thee surprised am I,
For now I love two women equally:
Both are well favored, both rich in array,
Which is the loveliest it is hard to say:
This seems the fairest, so doth that to me;
And this doth please me most, and so doth she;
Even as a boat tossed by contrary wind,
So with this love and that wavers my mind.
Venus, why doublest thou my endless smart?
Was not one wench enough to grieve my heart?
Why add'st thou stars to heaven, leaves to green woods,
And to the deep vast sea fresh water-floods?
Yet this is better far than lie alone:
Let such as be mine enemies have none;
Yea, let my foes sleep in an empty bed,
And in the midst their bodies largely spread:
But may soft love rouse up my drowsy eyes,
And from my mistress' bosom let me rise!
Let one wench cloy me with sweet love's delight.
If one can do't; if not, two every night.
Though I am slender, I have store of pith,
Nor want I strength, but weight, to press her with:
Pleasure adds fuel to my lustful fire,
I pay them home with that they most desire:

Oft have I spent the night in wantonness,
And in the morn been lively ne'ertheless.
He's happy who Love's mutual skirmish slays;
And to the gods for that death Ovid prays.
Let soldiers chase their enemies amain,
And with their blood eternal honour gain,
Let merchants seek wealth and with perjured lips,
Being wrecked, carouse the sea tired by their ships;
But when I die, would I might droop with doing,
And in the midst thereof, set my soul going,
That at my funeral some may weeping cry,
"Even as he led his life, so did he die."

Ovid
translated by Christopher Marlowe

Besides the long and elaborate narratives in The Canterbury Tales, Chaucer played with the shortest and tightest of French forms. In the brief and delicate rondel, he turned the tune so dexterously that it became a perfect English love song.

RONDEL OF MERCILESS BEAUTY

Your two great eyes will slay me suddenly;
Their beauty shakes me who was once serene;
Straight through my heart the wound is quick and keen.

Only your word will heal the injury
To my hurt heart, while yet the wound is clean—
　Your two great eyes will slay me suddenly;
　Their beauty shakes me who was once serene.

Upon my word, I tell you faithfully
Through life and after death you are my queen;
For with my death the whole truth shall be seen.
　Your two great eyes will slay me suddenly;
　Their beauty shakes me who was once serene;
　Straight through my heart the wound is quick and keen.

Geoffrey Chaucer
modern English version by Louis Untermeyer

Villon's roundel is a variation of Chaucer's rondel form. Both ring changes on repetition and alternation of rhymes, and both express themselves with a minimum of rhethoric.

ROUNDEL OF FAREWELL

Farewell, I say, with tearful eye.
  Farewell, the dearest sweet to see!
  Farewell, o'er all the kindest she!
Farewell, with heavy heart say I.
Farewell, my love, my soul, good-bye!
  My poor heart needs must part from thee:
Farewell, I say, with tearful eye.

Farewell, by whose default I die
  Deaths more than told of tongue can be;
  Farewell, of all the world to me
Whom most I blame and hold most high!
Farewell, I say, with tearful eye.

François Villon
translated by John Payne

THE FORSAKEN LOVER

They flee from me, that sometime did me seek,
With naked foot stalking within my chamber:
Once have I seen them gentle, tame, and meek,
That now are wild, and do not once remember,
That sometime they have put themselves in danger
To take bread at my hand; and now they range
Busily seeking with a continual change.

Thankéd be Fortune, it hath been otherwise
Twenty times better; but once in speciál,
In thin array, after a pleasant guise,
When her loose gown did from her shoulders fall,
And she me caught in her arms long and small,
And therewithal so sweetly did me kiss,
And softly said, "Dear heart, how like you this?"

It was no dream; for I lay broad awaking:
But all is turned now through my gentleness
Into a bitter fashion of forsaking,
And I have leave to go of her goodness,
And she also to use new-fangledness.
But since that I unkindly so am servéd,
"How like you this?"—What hath *she* now deservéd?

Sir Thomas Wyatt

Sir Philip Sidney wrote more than one hundred sonnets to Penelope Devereux, daughter of the Earl of Leicester. When they were assembled, he called the sequence Astrophil and Stella, a pun on his name: Philip, lover of a star. It is doubtful that Stella (Penelope) shared his passion. She married another, and Sidney became the husband of an heiress before he was twenty.

WITH HOW SAD STEPS, O MOON

With how sad steps, O Moon, thou climb'st the skies,
How silently, and with how wan a face!
What, may it be that even in heav'nly place
That busy archer his sharp arrows tries?
Sure, if that long-with-love-acquainted eyes
Can judge of love, thou feel'st a lover's case;
I read it in thy looks: thy languisht grace,
To me, that feel the like, thy state descries.
Then, ev'n of fellowship, O Moon, tell me,
Is constant love deem'd there but want of wit?
Are beauties there as proud as here they be?
Do they above love to be lov'd, and yet
Those lovers scorn whom that love doth possess?
Do they call virtue there ungratefulness?

Sir Philip Sidney

Little is known about the life of Michael Drayton although he left vast volumes of historical poetry, epistles in verse consisting of imaginary letters exchanged between famous couples, odes, satires, pastorals, and religious meditations. Nor is it certain who inspired the smoldering sonnet sequence, Idea's Mirror, nor what occasioned the anguished lines beginning "Since there's no help, come, let us kiss and part."

SINCE THERE'S NO HELP

Since there's no help, come, let us kiss and part.
Nay, I have done, you get no more of me!
And I am glad, yea, glad with all my heart,
That thus so cleanly I myself can free.
Shake hands for ever! Cancel all our vows!
And when we meet at any time again,
Be it not seen in either of our brows
That we one jot of former love retain.

Now at the last gasp of Love's latest breath,
When, his pulse failing, Passion speechless lies,
When Faith is kneeling by his bed of death,
And Innocence is closing up his eyes—
   Now, if thou would'st, when all have given him over,
   From death to life thou might'st him yet recover!

Michael Drayton

Among other felicities Shakespeare's Twelfth Night contains the most memorable image of unrequited love and the pathos of unhappy resignation. It is Viola's confession to the Duke who is not in love with her—she is disguised as a boy—but with the unresponsive Olivia.

SHE NEVER TOLD HER LOVE

. . . She never told her love,
But let concealment, like a worm i' the bud,
Feed on her damask cheek; she pined in thought
And with a green and yellow melancholy
She sat like patience on a monument,
Smiling at grief. Was not this love indeed?

William Shakespeare

SEALS OF LOVE

Take, O take those lips away
That so sweetly were forsworn,
And those eyes, the break of day,
Lights that do mislead the morn.
But my kisses bring again,
    Bring again—
Seals of love, but sealed in vain,
    Sealed in vain.

William Shakespeare

"Greensleeves" is one of the oldest and most popular of anguished love-songs. The airwaves carry it continually; today's boys and girls repeat it as though it were a recent hit tune. Yet it appeared almost four hundred years ago in a collection alluringly entitled A Handful of Pleasant Delights *(1584). Shakespeare liked the ballad well enough to quote it; there are two references to it in* The Merry Wives of Windsor. *Here are some of the original nineteen stanzas.*

GREENSLEEVES

Alas, my love, you do me wrong
    To cast me off discourteously;
And I have lovéd you so long,
    Delighting in your company.

Greensleeves was all my joy,
    Greensleeves was my delight:
Greensleeves was my heart of gold,
    And who but Lady Greensleeves.

I have been ready at your hand
    To grant whatever you would crave;
I have both wagéd life and land,
    Your love and good will for to have.

Greensleeves was all my joy, &c.

I bought thee kerchiefs for thy head,
    That were wrought fine and gallantly;
I kept thee both at board and bed,
    Which cost my purse well favoredly.

Greensleeves was all my joy, &c.

Thy crimson stockings all of silk,
    With gold all wrought above the knee;
Thy pumps as white as is the milk,
    And yet thou wouldst not love me.

Greensleeves was all my joy, &c.

My gayest gelding I thee gave,
    To ride wherever likéd thee;
No lady ever was so brave,
    And yet thou wouldst not love me.

Greensleeves was all my joy, &c.

Thou couldst desire no earthly thing,
    But still thou hadst it readily;
Thy music still to play and sing;
    And yet thou wouldst not love me.

Greensleeves was all my joy, &c.

Greensleeves, now farewell, adieu;
    God I pray to prosper thee;
For I am still thy lover true;
    Come once again and love me.

Greensleeves was all my joy,
    Greensleeves was my delight;
Greensleeves was my heart of gold,
    And who but Lady Greensleeves.

                    Clement Robinson

KIND ARE HER ANSWERS

Kind are her answers,
But her performance keeps no day;
Breaks time, as dancers
From their own music when they stray:
All her free favors
And smooth words wing my hopes in vain.
O did ever voice so sweet but only feign?
    Can true love yield such delay,
    Converting joy to pain?

Lost is our freedom,
When we submit to women so:
Why do we need 'em,
When in their best they work our woe?
There is no wisdom
Can alter ends, by Fate prefixed.
O why is the good of man with evil mixed?
　　Never were days yet calléd two,
But one night went betwixt.

Thomas Campion

BREAK OF DAY

Stay, O sweet, and do not rise;
The light that shines comes from thine eyes;
The day breaks not; it is my heart,
Because that you and I must part.
　　Stay, or else my joys will die
　　And perish in their infancy.

John Donne

SWEETEST LOVE, I DO NOT GO

Sweetest love, I do not go,
　　For weariness of thee,
Nor in hope the world can show
　　A fitter love for me;
　　　　But since that I
At the last must part, 'tis best,
Thus to use myself in jest
　　By feignéd deaths to die.

Yesternight the Sun went hence,
　　And yet is here to-day;
He hath no desire nor sense,
　　Nor half so short a way;
　　　　Then fear not me,
But believe that I shall make
Speedier journeys, since I take
　　More wings and spurs than he.

O how feeble is man's power,
   That if good fortune fall,
Cannot add another hour,
   Nor a lost hour recall;
     But come bad chance,
And we join it to our strength,
And we teach it art and length,
   Itself o'er us to advance.

When thou sigh'st, thou sigh'st not wind,
   But sigh'st my soul away;
When thou weep'st, unkindly kind,
   My life's blood doth decay.
     It cannot be
That thou lov'st me as thou say'st,
If in thine my life thou waste,
   That art the best of me.

Let not thy divining heart
   Forethink me any ill;
Destiny may take thy part,
   And may thy fears fulfil.
     But think that we
Are but turned aside to sleep;
They who one another keep
   Alive, ne'er parted be.

John Donne

SONG: HOW SWEET I ROAMED

How sweet I roamed from field to field
   And tasted all the summer's pride,
Till I the prince of love beheld
   Who in the sunny beams did glide!

He showed me lilies for my hair,
   And blushing roses for my brow;
He led me through his gardens fair
   Where all his golden pleasures grow.

With sweet May dews my wings were wet,
   And Phoebus fired my vocal rage;
He caught me in his silken net,
   And shut me in his golden cage.

He loves to sit and hear me sing,
   Then, laughing, sports and plays with me;
Then stretches out my golden wing,
   And mocks my loss of liberty.

William Blake

THE GARDEN OF LOVE

I went to the Garden of Love,
And saw what I never had seen:
A Chapel was built in the midst,
Where I used to play on the green.

And the gates of this Chapel were shut,
And "Thou shalt not" writ over the door;
So I turned to the Garden of Love
That so many sweet flowers bore;

And I saw it was filléd with graves.
And tombstones where flowers should be;
And priests in black gowns were walking their rounds,
And binding with briars my joys and desires.

William Blake

Robert Burns was anything but a "heaven-taught plowman," an ignorant son of the soil who knew nothing of poetic craft yet, somehow, became a national bard. He wrote in technically perfect English verse forms as well as in the rough Scottish dialect. But it is as maker (or adapter) of folk songs that Burns is beloved. He transformed the stereotypes of rustic life and the platitudes of love into fresh and imperishable lyrics.

Burns' "O Wert Thou in the Cauld Blast" and "Sweet Afton" can be found under "The Gallantry of Love" on pages 154 and 155.

THE BANKS O' DOON

Ye flowery banks o' bonie Doon,
    How can ye blume sae fair?
How can ye chant, ye little birds,
    And I sae fu' o' care!

Thou'll break my heart, thou bonie bird,
    That sings upon the bough!
Thou minds me o' the happy days
    When my fause luve was true.

Thou'll break my heart, thou bonie bird,
    That sings beside thy mate;
For sae I sat, and sae I sang,
    And wist na o' my fate.

Aft hae I rov'd by bonie Doon,
    To see the woodbine twine;
And ilka bird sang o' its luve,
    And sae did I o' mine.

Wi' lightsome heart I pu'd a rose,
    Upon its thorny tree;
But my fause luver staw[1] my rose,
    And left the thorn wi' me.

                                    Robert Burns

[1]Staw: stole.

AE FOND KISS

Ae fond kiss, and then we sever!
Ae fareweel, and then forever!
Deep in heart-wrung tears I'll pledge thee,
Warring sighs and groans I'll wage thee!

Who shall say that fortune grieves him,
While the star of hope she leaves him?
Me, nae cheerfu' twinkle lights me,
Dark despair around benights me.

I'll ne'er blame my partial fancy:
Naething could resist my Nancy!
But to see her was to love her,
Love but her, and love for ever.

Had we never lov'd sae kindly,
Had we never lov'd sae blindly,
Never met—or never parted—
We had ne'er been broken-hearted.

Fare thee weel, thou first and fairest!
Fare thee weel, thou best and dearest!
Thine be ilka joy and treasure,
Peace, enjoyment, love and pleasure!

Ae fond kiss, and then we sever!
Ae fareweel, alas, for ever!
Deep in heart-wrung tears I'll pledge thee,
Warring sighs and groans I'll wage thee!

Robert Burns

Keats' unconsummated love for Fanny Brawne broke out in some of
the most pitiful letters ever written. His passion, made all the more
frantic by frustration, was suppressed in several poems, but it cried out
in a sonnet that stammered with suffering, stumbled on in desperate
demand, and ended in a rush of pain. Rarely has there been a greater
and more pathetic concentration of agony.

"To Dream of Thee," a less anguished excerpt from Keats' "Lines
to Fanny," appears on page 165. The sonnet "Bright Star," which Fanny
Brawne copied into Keats' pocket Dante, is on page 204.

I CRY YOUR MERCY

I cry your mercy—pity—love—aye, love!
  Merciful love that tantalizes not,
One-thoughted, never-wandering, guileless love,
  Unmasked, and being seen, without a blot!
O! let me have thee whole—all—all—be mine!
  That shape, that fairness, that sweet minor zest
Of love, your kiss—those hands, those eyes divine,
  That warm, white, lucent, million-pleasured breast—
Yourself—your soul—in pity give me all.
  Withhold no atom's atom or I die,
Or living on perhaps, your wretched thrall,
  Forget, in the mist of idle misery,
Life's purposes—the palate of my mind
Losing its gust, and my ambition blind!

John Keats

Unlike Keats' anguish, Byron's sounds theatrical; it is too melodius for misery. His poems brim with tears, grief, and passion, but, in Byron's fluent verse, they seem standard properties rather than inevitable expressions of deeply stirred emotions. Nevertheless, they make a lingering music.

WE'LL GO NO MORE A-ROVING

So, we'll go no more a-roving
  So late into the night,
Though the heart be still as loving,
  And the moon be still as bright.

For the sword outwears its sheath,
  And the soul wears out the breast,
And the heart must pause to breathe,
  And love itself have rest.

Though the night was made for loving,
  And the day returns too soon,
Yet we'll go no more a-roving
  By the light of the moon.

George Gordon, Lord Byron

WHEN WE TWO PARTED

When we two parted
  In silence and tears,
Half broken-hearted
  To sever for years,
Pale grew thy cheek and cold,
  Colder thy kiss;
Truly that hour foretold
  Sorrow to this.

The dew of the morning
  Sunk chill on my brow—
It felt like the warning
  Of what I feel now.
Thy vows are all broken,
  And light is thy fame;
I hear thy name spoken,
  And share in its shame.

They name thee before me,
  A knell to mine ear;
A shudder comes o'er me—
  Why wert thou so dear?
They know not I knew thee,
  Who knew thee too well:—
Long, long shall I rue thee,
  Too deeply to tell.

In secret we met—
  In silence I grieve
That thy heart could forget,
  Thy spirit deceive.
If I should meet thee
  After long years,
How should I greet thee?—
  With silence and tears.

George Gordon, Lord Byron

FAREWELL!

Farewell! if ever fondest prayer
   For other's weal availed on high,
Mine will not all be lost in air,
   But waft thy name beyond the sky.
'Twere vain to speak, to weep, to sigh:
   Oh! more than tears of blood can tell,
When wrung from guilt's expiring eye,
   Are in that word—Farewell!—Farewell!

These lips are mute, these eyes are dry;
   But in my breast and in my brain,
Awake the pangs that pass not by,
   The thought that ne'er shall sleep again.
My soul nor deigns nor dares complain,
   Though grief and passion there rebel:
I only know we loved in vain;
   I only feel—Farewell!—Farewell!

George Gordon, Lord Byron

Son of two actors, himself a bewildered actor in a life that ended in melodramatic tragedy, Edgar Allan Poe was instinctively drawn to the morbidly theatrical. His best work mixed reality with unreality; his fiction is a panorama of fantasy, and his poetry, out of space, out of time, moves like a wavering dream.

Poe's exquisite "To Helen" is on page 168.

A DREAM WITHIN A DREAM

Take this kiss upon the brow!
And, in parting from you now,
Thus much let me avow—
You are not wrong, who deem
That my days have been a dream;
Yet if Hope has flown away
In a night, or in a day,
In a vision, or in none,
Is it therefore the less gone?
All that we see or seem
Is but a dream within a dream.

I stand amid the roar
Of a surf-tormented shore,
And I hold within my hand
Grains of the golden sand—
How few! yet how they creep
Through my fingers to the deep,
While I weep—while I weep!
O God! can I not grasp
Them with a tighter clasp?
O God! can I not save
One from the pitiless wave?
Is *all* that we see or seem
But a dream within a deam?

Edgar Allan Poe

As a person, the nineteenth-century Walter Savage Landor was eccentric, quarrelsome, violent, and ridiculously disorganized. As a poet, however, he was an unusually restrained craftsman whose work breathed a classical calm. The lyric that follows is so simple as to appear foolish, yet it is perfect in its seeming artlessness and poignant in its very naïveté.

MOTHER, I CANNOT MIND MY WHEEL

Mother, I cannot mind my wheel;
    My fingers ache, my lips are dry.
O, if you felt the pain I feel!
    But O, who ever felt as I!

No longer could I doubt him true—
    All other men may use deceit—
He always said my eyes were blue,
    And often swore my lips were sweet.

Walter Savage Landor

Tennyson's The Princess is a curious blend of propaganda and pure music. Its subject was the then controversial "woman question" and Tennyson maintained that women could not be liberated by a higher education because of their biological limitation. The priggishness of that thesis was burlesqued by Gilbert and Sullivan in *Princess Ida*, which they called "a respectful operatic perversion." Today *The Princess* is read (when it is read at all) only for its interludes and its lyrics, such as the following.

ASK ME NO MORE

Ask me no more. The moon may draw the sea;
  The cloud may stoop from heaven and take the shape,
  With fold to fold, of mountain or of cape;
But O too fond, when have I answered thee?
    Ask me no more..

Ask me no more. What answer should I give?
  I love not hollow cheek or faded eye;
  Yet, O my friend, I will not have thee die!
Ask me no more, lest I should bid thee live;
    Ask me no more.

Ask me no more. Thy fate and mine are sealed;
  I strove against the stream and all in vain;
  Let the great river take me to the main.
No more, dear love, for at a touch I yield;
    Ask me no more.

Alfred, Lord Tennyson

Emily Dickinson, greatest of all women poets, spent practically her entire life in the house in which she was born and in which she died. Nothing disturbed her seclusion in her Amherst, Massachusetts, home except one thing: the deepest emotion which she kept repressed. In her early twenties something happened which changed the happy girl into a pathetic solitary. She heard a sermon and fell in love with the preacher. He was married, completely unaware of the feeling he had stirred in the heart of his listener. Emily knew that he could not love her and that she could never love anyone else.

The love that could not be fulfilled found expression in poem after poem. Devotion and despair, wildness and vain wishes, anguish and abnegation suffuse the lines that Emily Dickinson wrote to ease her pain—lines that compose some of the most poignant lyrics ever written.

THE SOUL SELECTS HER OWN SOCIETY

The soul selects her own society,
Then shuts the door;
On her divine majority
Obtrude no more.

Unmoved, she notes the chariot's pausing
At her low gate;
Unmoved, an emperor is kneeling
Upon her mat.

I've known her from an ample nation
Choose one;
Then close the valves of her attention
Like stone.

Emily Dickinson

I HAVE NO LIFE BUT THIS

I have no life but this,
To lead it here;
Nor any death, but lest
Dispelled from there;

Nor tie to earths to come,
Nor action new,
Except through this extent,
The realm of you.

Emily Dickinson

COME SLOWLY, EDEN!

Come slowly, Eden!
Lips unused to thee,
Bashful, sip thy jasmines,
As the fainting bee,
Reaching late his flower,
Round her chamber hums,
Counts his nectars—enters—
And is lost in balms!

Emily Dickinson

I CANNOT LIVE WITH YOU

I cannot live with you,
It would be life,
And life is over there
Behind the shelf

The sexton keeps the key to,
Putting up
Our life, his porcelain,
Like a cup

Discarded of the housewife,
Quaint or broke;
A newer Sèvres pleases,
Old ones crack.

I could not die with you,
For one must wait
To shut the other's gaze down,—
You could not.

And I, could I stand by
And see you freeze,
Without my right of frost,
Death's privilege?

Nor could I rise with you,
Because your face
Would put out Jesus',
That new grace

Glow plain and foreign
On my homesick eye,
Except that you, than he
Shone closer by.

They'd judge us—how?
For you served Heaven, you know,
Or sought to;
I could not,

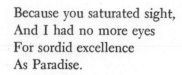

Because you saturated sight,
And I had no more eyes
For sordid excellence
As Paradise.

And were you lost, I would be,
Though my name
Rang loudest
On the heavenly fame.

And were you saved,
And I condemned to be
Where you were not,
That self were hell to me.

So we must keep apart,
You there, I here,
With just the door ajar
That oceans are,
And prayer,
And that pale sustenance,
Despair!

Emily Dickinson

OF ALL THE SOULS THAT STAND CREATE

Of all the souls that stand create
I have elected one.
When sense from spirit files away,
And subterfuge is done;

When that which is and that which was
Apart, intrinsic, stand,
And this brief tragedy of flesh
Is shifted like a sand;

When figures show their royal front
And mists are carved away—
Behold the atom I preferred
To all the lists of clay!

Emily Dickinson

MINE

Mine by the right of the white election!
Mine by the royal seal!
Mine by the sign in the scarlet prison
Bars cannot conceal!

Mine, here in vision and in veto!
Mine, by the grave's repeal
Titled, confirmed,—delirious charter!
Mine, while the ages steal!

Emily Dickinson

WILD NIGHTS

Wild nights! Wild nights!
Were I with thee,
Wild nights should be
Our luxury!

Futile the winds
To a heart in port—
Done with the compass,
Done with the chart.

Rowing in Eden!
Ah! the sea!
Might I but moor
Tonight in thee!

Emily Dickinson

MY LIFE CLOSED TWICE

My life closed twice before its close;
It yet remains to see
If Immortality unveil
A third event to me,

So huge, so hopeless to conceive,
As these that twice befell.
Parting is all we know of heaven,
And all we need of hell.

Emily Dickinson

Like Emily Dickinson (see page 85), Christina Rossetti withdrew from the world. She, too, could not surrender herself to love. Also, as with Emily Dickinson, the denial of love was responsible for her most moving poems. Longing, unhappy memories, and heartbreak well up from dozens of her songs and sonnets, notably from "The Hope I Dreamed Of," "Remember Me," "Song: When I Am Dead," and the bitter-sweet "Echo."

Other poems by Christina Rossetti are on pages 8 and 137.

THE HOPE I DREAMED OF

The hope I dreamed of was a dream,
  Was but a dream. And now I wake
Exceeding comfortless, and worn, and old,
  For a dream's sake.

I hang my harp upon a tree,
  A weeping willow in a lake;
I hang my silenced harp there, wrung and snapt,
  For a dream's sake.

Lie still, lie still, my breaking heart;
  My silent heart, lie still and break.
Life, and the world, and mine own self, are changed
  For a dream's sake.

Christina Rossetti

REMEMBER ME

Remember me when I am gone away,
Gone far away into the silent land;
When you can no more hold me by the hand,
Nor I half turn to go, yet, turning, stay.
Remember me when no more, day by day,
You tell me of our future that you planned.
Only remember me; you understand
It will be late to counsel then or pray.

Yet if you should forget me for a while
And afterwards remember, do not grieve;
For if the darkness and corruption leave
A vestige of the thoughts that once I had,
Better by far you should forget and smile
Than that you should remember and be sad.

Christina Rossetti

SONG: WHEN I AM DEAD

When I am dead, my dearest,
    Sing no sad songs for me;
Plant thou no roses at my head,
    Nor shady cypress-tree:
Be the green grass above me
    With showers and dewdrops wet;
And if thou wilt, remember,
    And if thou wilt, forget.

I shall not see the shadows,
    I shall not feel the rain;
I shali not hear the nightingale
    Sing on, as if in pain:
And dreaming through the twilight
    That doth not rise nor set,
Haply I may remember,
    And haply may forget.

Christina Rossetti

ECHO

Come to me in the silence of the night;
Come in the speaking silence of a dream;
Come with soft rounded cheeks and eyes as bright
As sunlight on a stream;
Come back in tears,
O memory, hope, love of finished years.

91

O dream how sweet, too sweet, too bitter-sweet,
Whose wakening should have been in Paradise,
Where souls brim-full of love abide and meet;
Where thirsting longing eyes
Watch the slow door
That opening, letting in, lets out no more.

Yet come to me in dreams, that I may live
My very life again though cold in death;
Come back to me in dreams, that I may give
Pulse for pulse, breath for breath:
Speak low, lean low,
As long ago my love, how long ago.

Christina Rossetti

Thrice-married Coventry Patmore was the unofficial laureate of con-
nubial domesticity. His volume The Angel in the House, with its
glorification of the wifely "rapture of submission," delighted readers
because of its prim and sometimes ridiculous details of a Victorian
courtship. Far different is Patmore's The Unknown Eros which, some-
how, combined eroticism with mysticism in a celebration of spiritual
love. Of the two poems which follow, the first is from The Unknown
Eros, the second is from The Angel in the House.

A FAREWELL

With all my will, but much against my heart,
We two now part.
My Very Dear,
Our solace is, the sad road lies so clear.
It needs no art,
With faint, averted feet
And many a tear,
In our opposéd paths to persevere.
Go thou to East, I West.
We will not say
There's any hope, it is so far away.
But, O my Best,
When the one darling of our widowhead,
The nursling Grief,
Is dead.

And no dews blur our eyes
To see the peach-bloom come in evening skies,
Perchance we may,
Where now this night is day,
And even through faith of still averted feet,
Making full circle of our banishment,
Amazéd meet;
The bitter journey to the bourne so sweet
Seasoning the termless feast of our content
With tears of recognition never dry.

Coventry Patmore

THE MARRIED LOVER

Why, having won her, do I woo?
  Because her spirit's vestal grace
Provokes me always to pursue,
  But, spirit-like, eludes embrace. . . .

Because, although in act and word
  As lowly as a wife can be,
Her manners, when they call me lord,
  Remind me 'tis by courtesy.

Because her gay and lofty brows,
  When all is won which hope can ask,
Reflect a light of hopeless snows
  That bright in virgin ether bask;

Because, tho' free of the outer court
  I am, this Temple keeps its shrine
Sacred to Heaven; because, in short,
  She's not and never can be mine.

Coventry Patmore

Beginning as a professional architect, Thomas Hardy found more pleasure composing poems. When publishers declined his poetry, he turned to novel-writing. Under The Greenwood Tree, Far from the Madding Crowd, and several other novels were rated as masterpieces. When Tess of the D'Urbervilles was condemned by the ultra-religious and Jude the Obscure was castigated as revolting, Hardy returned to poetry, especially to the conversational style that anticipated the "everyday syntax" of modern poetry.

NEUTRAL TONES

We stood by a pond that winter day,
And the sun was white, as though chidden of God,
And a few leaves lay on the starving sod;
    They had fallen from an ash, and were gray.

Your eyes on me were as eyes that rove
Over tedious riddles solved years ago;
And some words played between us to and fro
    On which lost the more by our love.

The smile on your mouth was the deadest thing
Alive enough to have strength to die;
And a grin of bitterness swept thereby
    Like an ominous bird a-wing. . . .

Since then, keen lessons that love deceives,
And wrings with wrong, have shaped to me
Your face, and the God-curst sun, and a tree,
    And a pond edged with grayish leaves.

                                        Thomas Hardy

SING, BALLAD-SINGER

Sing, ballad-singer, raise a hearty tune;
Make me forget that there was ever a one
I walked with in the meek light of the moon
        When the day's work was done.

Rhyme, ballad-rhymer, start a country song;
Make me forget that she whom I loved well
Swore she would love me dearly, love me long.
        Then—what I cannot tell!

Sing, ballad-singer, from your little book;
Make me forget those heart-breaks, achings, fears;
Make me forget her name, her sweet, sweet look.
Make me forget her tears.

Thomas Hardy

Although she did not live beyond her twenty-eighth year, Amy Levy left a few precious lyrics for grief-stricken lovers. "June" is one of the loveliest.

JUNE

Last June I saw your face three times,
Three times I touched your hand;
Now, as before, May month is o'er,
And June is in the land.

O many Junes shall come and go,
Flower-footed o'er the mead;
O many Junes for me, to whom
Is length of days decreed.

There shall be sunlight, scent of rose,
Warm mist of Summer rain;
Only this change—I shall not look
Upon your face again.

Amy Levy

In 1887, when she was twenty-two, Adela Florence Cory left England to join her parents in India. There she fell in love and married Malcolm Nicolson who, besides being an expert linguist, was a colonel in the Bengal Army. She spent much of her time writing love poetry, poetry that was so impassioned that, fearing Victorian condemnation, she adopted a masculine pen-name, Laurence Hope. Her Songs from the Garden of Kama and Indian Love Lyrics were set to music, and there were few drawing-rooms that did not quiver with "Pale Hands I Loved Beside the Shalimar," and "Less Than the Dust." Her husband died in a nursing home and she refused to survive him. Two months after his death, while still in her thirties, she killed herself by swallowing a dose of mercury.

LESS THAN THE DUST

Less than the dust beneath thy chariot wheel,
Less than the rust that never stained thy sword,
Less than the trust thou hast in me, O Lord,
                              Even less than these!

Less than the weed that grows beside thy door,
Less than the speed of hours spent far from thee,
Less than the need thou hast in life of me.
                              Even less am I.

Since I, O Lord, am nothing unto thee,
See here thy sword, I make it keen and bright,
Love's last reward, Death, comes to me to-night,
                              Farewell, Zahir-u-din.

                                        Laurence Hope

96

Living for a while in the East End of London where his father owned a dry dock, Ernest Dowson fell in love with the daughter of a restaurant keeper. It was a platonic love, and the girl could not understand either Dowson's reticent idealism nor the poem he wrote to her. Its title was Non Sum Qualis Eram Bonae Sub Regno Cynarae ("I am not what I was during the reign of the lovely Cynara"), a line which Dowson had taken from Horace. This classic of sentimental decadence was wasted on his "Cynara"; she ran off and married one of her father's waiters.

FAITHFUL IN MY FASHION

Last night, ah, yesternight, betwixt her lips and mine
There fell thy shadow, Cynara! thy breath was shed
Upon my soul between the kisses and the wine;
And I was desolate and sick of an old passion,
   Yea, I was desolate and bowed my head:
I have been faithful to thee, Cynara! in my fashion.

All night upon mine heart I felt her warm heart beat,
Night-long within mine arms in love and sleep she lay;
Surely the kisses of her bought red mouth were sweet;
But I was desolate and sick of an old passion,
   When I awoke and found the dawn was gray:
I have been faithful to thee, Cynara! in my fashion.

I have forgot much, Cynara! gone with the wind,
Flung roses, roses riotously with the throng,
Dancing, to put thy pale, lost lilies out of mind;
But I was desolate and sick of an old passion,
   Yea, all the time, because the dance was long:
I have been faithful to thee, Cynara! in my fashion.

I cried for madder music and for stronger wine,
But when the feast is finished and the lamps expire,
Then falls thy shadow, Cynara! the night is thine;
And I am desolate and sick of an old passion,
   Yea, hungry for the lips of my desire:
I have been faithful to thee, Cynara! in my fashion.

Ernest Dowson

There is enchantment in everything by William Butler Yeats. The early lyrics are otherworldy with landscapes lit by twilight; nowhere is the visionary poet heard with more magic than in the sad music of "When You are Old."

WHEN YOU ARE OLD

When you are old and gray and full of sleep,
And nodding by the fire, take down this book,
And slowly read, and dream of the soft look
Your eyes had once, and of their shadows deep;

How many loved your moments of glad grace,
And loved your beauty with love false or true;
But one man loved the pilgrim soul in you,
And loved the sorrows of your changing face.

And bending down beside the glowing bars
Murmur, a little sadly, how love fled
And paced upon the mountains overhead
And hid his face amid a crowd of stars.

William Butler Yeats

Selections from Housman's A Shropshire Lad appear on pages 55 - 56. A more somber mood intensifies the next two poems from the same sequence. The tone deepens from the sad soliloquy of "White in the Moon" to the tragic irony of "Bredon Hill."

WHITE IN THE MOON

White in the moon the long road lies,
The moon stands blank above;
White in the moon the long road lies
That leads me from my love.

Still hangs the hedge without a gust,
Still, still the shadows stay:
My feet upon the moonlit dust
Pursue the ceaseless way.

The world is round, so travelers tell,
And straight though reach the track,
Trudge on, trudge on, 'twill all be well,
The way will guide one back.

But ere the circle homeward hies
Far, far it must remove:
White in the moon the long road lies
That leads me from my love.

A. E. Housman

BREDON HILL

In summertime on Bredon
    The bells they sound so clear;
Round both the shires they ring them
    In steeples far and near,
    A happy noise to hear.

Here of a Sunday morning
    My love and I would lie,
And see the coloured counties,
    And hear the larks so high
    About us in the sky.

The bells would ring to call her
    In valleys miles away:
"Come all to church, good people;
    Good people, come and pray."
    But here my love would stay.

And I would turn and answer
    Among the springing thyme,
"Oh, peal upon our wedding,
    And we will hear the chime,
    And come to church in time."

But when the snows at Christmas
    On Bredon top were strown,
My love rose up so early
    And stole out unbeknown
    And went to church alone.

They tolled the one bell only,
    Groom there was none to see,
The mourners followed after,
    And so to church went she,
    And would not wait for me.

The bells they sound on Bredon,
    And still the steeples hum,
"Come all to church, good people"—
    Oh, noisy bells, be dumb;
    I hear you; I will come.

A. E. Housman

The next four poems reflect different attitudes of pain and sorrow. The first two are by an Englishwoman who never attained the popular esteem which she merited; the other two are by twentieth-century American poets. All are deep-felt and, each in its own way, penetrating.

SEA LOVE

Tide be runnin' the great world over:
    'Twas only last June month I mind that we
Was thinkin' the toss and the call in the breast of the lover
    So everlastin' as the sea.

Here's the same little fishes that sputter and swim,
    Wi' the moon's old glim on the gray, wet sand;
An' him no more to me nor me to him
    Than the wind goin' over my hand.

Charlotte Mew

I HAVE BEEN THROUGH THE GATES

His heart, to me, was a place of palaces and pinnacles and shining towers;
I saw it then as we see things in dreams,—I do not remember how long
    I slept;
I remember the trees, and the high, white walls, and how the sun was
    always on the towers;
The walls are standing today, and the gates: I have been through the
    gates, I have groped, I have crept
Back, back. There is dust in the streets, and blood; they are empty;
    darkness is over them;
His heart is a place with the lights gone out, forsaken by great winds
    and the heavenly rain, unclean and unswept,
Like the heart of the holy city, old, blind, beautiful Jerusalem,
Over which Christ wept.

Charlotte Mew

LOVE SONG FROM NEW ENGLAND

In every solemn tree the wind
    Has rung a little lonesome bell,
As sweet and clear, as cool and kind
    As my voice bidding you farewell.

This is an hour that gods have loved
    To snatch with bare, bright hands and hold.
Mine, with a gesture, grey and gloved,
    Dismiss it from me in the cold.

Closely as some dark-shuttered house
    I keep my light. How should you know,
That as you turn beneath brown boughs,
    My heart is breaking in the snow.

Winifred Welles

Edna St. Vincent Millay was famous at nineteen; her long, mystical poem "Renascence," submitted in an anthology contest, failed to win a prize but was the only contribution remembered, repeated, and continually reprinted. Sixteen volumes of poems and plays established her reputation as one who could express the perennial mutations of love with wit as well as passion. No poet of the period was more quoted; no anthology was complete without a Millay sonnet as poignant as the one which follows.

WHAT LIPS MY LIPS HAVE KISSED

What lips my lips have kissed, and where, and why,
I have forgotten, and what arms have lain
Under my head till morning; but the rain
Is full of ghosts tonight, that tap and sigh
Upon the glass and listen for reply;
And in my heart there stirs a quiet pain
For unremembered lads that not again
Will turn to me at midnight with a cry.

Thus in the winter stands the lonely tree,
Nor knows what birds have vanished one by one,
Yet knows its boughs more silent than before:
I cannot say what loves have come and gone;
I only know that summer sang in me
A little while, that in me sings no more.

Edna St. Vincent Millay

FOLK-SONG

Back she came through the trembling dusk;
  And her mother spoke and said:
"What is it makes you late today,
And why do you smile and sing as gay
  As though you just were wed?"
"Oh, mother, my hen that never had chicks
  Has hatched out six!"

Back she came through the flaming dusk;
  And her mother spoke and said:
"What gives your eyes that dancing light,
What makes your lips so strangely bright,
  And why are your cheeks so red?"
"Oh, mother, the berries I ate in the lane
  Have left a stain."

102

Back she came through the faltering dusk;
   And her mother spoke and said:
"You are weeping; your footstep is heavy with care—
What makes you totter and cling to the stair,
   And why do you hang your head?"
"Oh, mother—oh, mother—you never can know.
   I loved him so!"

Louis Untermeyer

Few poets have explored the limits of levity and gravity as daringly as W. H. Auden. He has written clerihews and limericks as well as some of the most solemnly meditative poetry of the period. "Stop All the Clocks" uses seemingly incompatible and curiously whimsical ideas— "crêpe bows round the white necks of the public doves," policemen with black cotton gloves, announcement of death by sky-writers—to create arresting metaphors of grief.

STOP ALL THE CLOCKS

Stop all the clocks, cut off the telephone,
Prevent the dog from barking with a juicy bone,
Silence the pianos and with muffled drum
Bring out the coffin, let the mourners come.

Let aeroplanes circle moaning overhead
Scribbling on the sky the message He Is Dead,
Put crêpe bows round the white necks of the public doves,
Let the traffic policemen wear black cotton gloves.

He was my North, my South, my East and West,
My working week and my Sunday rest,
My noon, my midnight, my talk, my song;
I thought that love would last for ever. I was wrong.

The stars are not wanted now; put out every one:
Pack up the moon and dismantle the sun;
Pour away the ocean and sweep up the woods:
For nothing now can ever come to any good.

W. H. Auden

Kenneth Fearing was celebrated for his novels of suspense, but his poetry is more exciting than his prose. Discarding what he called "the entire bag of conventions usually associated with poetry," Fearing exposed his characters—gangsters, prostitutes, businessmen, cab drivers, quarreling lovers—against a background of neon lights that light up and distort the metropolitan scene.

LOVE 20¢ THE FIRST QUARTER MILE

All right. I may have lied to you and about you, and made a few
    pronouncements a bit too sweeping, perhaps, and possibly forgotten
    to tag the bases here or there,
And damned your extravagance, and maligned your tastes, and libeled
    your relatives, and slandered a few of your friends,
O.K.,
Nevertheless, come back.

Come home. I will agree to forget the statements that you issued so
    copiously to the neighbors and the press,
And you will forget that figment of your imagination, the blonde from
    Detroit;
I will agree that your lady friend who lives above us is not crazy, bats,
    nutty as they come, but on the contrary rather bright,
And you will concede that poor old Steinberg is neither a drunk, nor
    a swindler, but simply a guy, on the eccentric side, trying to get along.
(Are you listening, you bitch, and have you got this straight?)

Because I forgive you, yes, for everything.
I forgive you for being beautiful and generous and wise,
I forgive you, to put it simply, for being alive, and pardon you, in short,
    for being you.

Because tonight you are in my hair and eyes,
And every street light that our taxi passes shows me you again, still you,
And because tonight all other nights are black, all other hours are cold
    and far away, and now, this minute, the stars are very near and bright

Come back. We will have a celebration to end all celebrations.
We will invite the undertaker who lives beneath us, and a couple of
    boys from the office, and some other friends.
And Steinberg, who is off the wagon, and that insane woman who lives
    upstairs, and a few reporters, if anything should break.

Kenneth Fearing

Few poems have been written about the after-effects of divorce. "Mementos" is such a poem. It registers the feeling of frustrated lives —"we drained out one another's force"—while an old photograph and a dress worn to a dance recall memories sharpened by a lingering love. The tone of the poem is casual but, beneath the offhand manner, there is the sudden stab of regret.

MEMENTOS

Sorting out letters and piles of my old
    Cancelled checks, old clippings, and yellow note cards
That meant something once, I happened to find
    Your picture. *That* picture. I stopped there cold,
Like a man raking piles of dead leaves in his yard
      Who has turned up a severed hand.

Yet, that first second, I was glad: you stand
    Just as you stood—shy, delicate, slender,
In the long gown of green lace netting and daisies
    That you wore to our first dance. The sight of you stunned
Us all. Our needs seemed simpler, then;
      And our ideals came easy.

Then through the war and those two long years
    Overseas, the Japanese dead in their shacks
Among dishes, dolls, and lost shoes—I carried
    This glimpse of you, there, to choke down my fear,
Prove it had been, that it might come back.
      That was before we got married.

—Before we drained out one another's force
    With lies, self-denial, unspoken regret
And the sick eyes that blame; before the divorce
    And the treachery. Say it: before we met.
Still, I put back your picture. Someday, in due course,
      I will find that it's still there.

W. D. Snodgrass

A young British poet, Jon Stallworthy delighted readers with his blend of the casual and the symbolic. "Elegy for a Mis-spent Youth" is a swift yet subtle commentary on the times.

ELEGY FOR A MIS-SPENT YOUTH

Now that the chestnut candles burn
for your birthday, thickening the air
with vapoured sap, my thoughts return
to the attic over the square,
the table with its open book
and a bottle in which the red
sun set, your dress over the back
of a chair, and the bed
where, nightly, drowsy with the fair
exchange of love and with the smell
of chestnut wicks lighting the square,
we never lay and never shall.

Jon Stallworthy

The following poem is a virelay, one of the more uncommon of the French forms.

FINIS?

Since now, at last, we understand,
    Why all this feigned surprise?
No time for being blind and bland.
    Open your eyes.

I learned suspicion and surmise,
    Flourished on false alarms,
Fed by deceits and lulled by lies,
    Even in your arms.

Impervious to threatening storms,
    We trifled, hand in glove.
Gone are the lures, the whispered charms.
    I've had enough.

And yet . . . are we past thinking of
    What might be rescued, and
Restored with—shall I say it?—love?
    Give me your hand.

Michael Lewis

The
Drama
of
Love

$\mathbf{M}$ore intense and often more intolerable than the pains of passion are the dramas of love. Betrayal and bloodshed are compact in such early ballads as "Lord Randal," "The Douglas Tragedy," and "Barbara Allen." The reader responds swiftly to Browning's dramatic meetings and partings, moved by the pangs of separation and the joys of reunion, by the mad violence of "Porphyria's Lover" and the unfulfilled longings of "Two in the Campagna," with the

> Infinite passion and the pain
> Of finite hearts that yearn.

Drama is also the keynote of Matthew Arnold's somber and impassioned "Dover Beach." It is implicit in the conflict between decorum and desire in Anna Wickham's "The Fired Poet." It breaks through the seemingly casual quatrains of Housman's "Is My Team Ploughing" and prepares the grim ending of "The True Lover."

LORD RANDAL

"O where hae ye been, Lord Randal, my son?
O where hae ye been, my handsome young man?"
"I hae been to the wild wood; mother, make my bed soon,
For I'm weary wi' hunting, and fain wald lie down."

"Where gat ye your dinner, Lord Randal, my son?
Where gat ye your dinner, my handsome young man?"
"I dined wi' my true-love; mother, make my bed soon,
For I'm weary wi' hunting, and fain wald lie down."

"What gat ye to your dinner, Lord Randal, my son?
What gat ye to your dinner, my handsome young man?"
"I gat eels boil'd in broth; mother, make my bed soon,
For I'm weary wi' hunting, and fain wald lie down."

"What became of your bloodhounds, Lord Randal, my son?
What became of your bloodhounds, my handsome young man?"
"O they swell'd and they died; mother, make my bed soon,
For I'm weary wi' hunting, and fain wald lie down."

"O I fear ye are poison'd, Lord Randal, my son!
O I fear ye are poison'd, my handsome young man!"
"O yes! I am poison'd; mother, make my bed soon,
For I'm sick at the heart, and I fain wald lie down."

Anonymous

THE DOUGLAS TRAGEDY

"Rise up, rise up, now, Lord Douglas," she says,
  "And put on your armor so bright;
Let it never be said that a daughter of thine
  Was married to a lord under night.

"Rise up, rise up, my seven bold sons,
  And put on your armor so bright,
And take better care of your youngest sister,
  For your eldest's awa' last night."

Lady Margret was on a milk-white steed,
  Lord William was on a grey,
With a bugelet horn hung down by his side,
  And lightly they rode away.

Lord William lookit o'er his left shoulder,
  To see what he could see,
And there he spy'd her seven brethren bold,
  Come riding o'er the lee.

"Light down, light down, Lady Margret," he said,
  "And hold my steed in your hand,
Until that against your seven brethren bold,
  And your father, I make a stand."

She held his steed in her milk-white hand,
  And never shed one tear,
Until that she saw her seven brethren fa',
  And her father hard fighting, who loved her so dear.

"O hold your hand, Lord William!" she said,
  "For your strokes they are wondrous sair;
True lovers I can get many a ane,
  But a father I can never get mair."

O she's ta'en out her handkerchief,
　　It was o' the holland sae fine,
And aye she bound up her father's bloody wounds,
　　That were redder than the wine.

"O chuse, O chuse, Lady Margret," he said,
　　"O whether will ye gang or bide?"
"I'll gang, I'll gang, Lord William," she said,
　　"For you have left me no other guide."

He's lifted her on a milk-white steed,
　　And himself on a dapple grey,
With a bugelet horn hung down by his side,
　　And slowly they baith rade away.

O they rade on, and on they rade,
　　And a' by the light of the moon,
Until they came to yon wan water,
　　And there they lighted down.

They lighted down to take a drink
  Of the spring that ran sae clear,
And down the stream ran his gude heart's blood,
  And sair she 'gan to fear.

"Hold up, hold up, Lord William," she says,
  "For I fear that you are slain!"
" 'Tis naething but the shadow of my scarlet cloak,
  That shines in the water sae plain."

O they rade on, and on they rade,
  And a' by the light of the moon,
Until they cam to his mother's ha' door,
  And there they lighted down.

"Get up, get up, lady mother," he says,
  "Get up, and let me in!
Get up, get up, lady mother," he says,
  "For this night my fair lady I've win.

"O make my bed, lady mother," he says,
  "O make it braid and deep!
And lay Lady Margret close at my back,
  And the sounder I will sleep."

Lord William was dead lang ere midnight,
  Lady Margret lang ere day,
And all true lovers that go thegither,
  May they have mair luck than they!

Lord William was buried in St. Marie's kirk,
  Lady Margret in Marie's quire;
Out o' the lady's grave grew a bonny red rose,
  And out o' the knight's a brier.

And they twa met, and they twa plat,[1]
  And fain they wad be near;
And a' the warld might ken right weel
  They were twa lovers dear.

                                        Anonymous

[1]Plat: grew together.

"Barbara Allen" (sometimes called "The Cruelty of Barbara Allen") is one of the oldest and saddest of romantic ballads—it is said that Oliver Goldsmith wept whenever he heard it. When it was transplanted from England to America it grew in popularity as well as variety. In Virginia alone there exist more than ninety different variations of the song about the hopeless lover and the hard-hearted girl. The following version is one most often heard.

BARBARA ALLEN

All in the merry month of May,
　　When green buds they were swelling,
Young Jemmy Grove on his death-bed lay
　　For love of Barbara Allen.

He sent his man unto her then,
　　To the town where she was dwelling:
"O haste and come to my master dear,
　　If your name be Barbara Allen."

Slowly, slowly she rose up,
　　And she came where he was lying;
And when she drew the curtain by,
　　Says, "Young man, I think you're dying."

"O it's I am sick, and very, very sick,
　　And it's all for Barbara Allen."
"O the better for me you'll never be,
　　Tho' your heart's blood were a-spilling!

"O do you not mind, young man," she says,
　　"When the red wine you were filling,
That you made the healths go round and round,
　　And slighted Barbara Allen?"

He turned his face unto the wall,
　　And death with him was dealing:
"Adieu, adieu, my dear friends all;
　　Be kind to Barbara Allen."

As she was walking o'er the fields,
    She heard the dead-bell knelling;
And every toll the dead-bell struck,
    Cried, "Woe to Barbara Allen!"

"O mother, mother, make my bed,
    To lay me down in sorrow.
My love has died for me today,
    I'll die for him tomorrow."

Anonymous

THE LOST MISTRESS

All's over, then: does truth sound bitter
    As one at first believes?
Hark, 'tis the sparrows' good-night twitter
    About your cottage eaves!

And the leaf-buds on the vine are woolly,
    I noticed that, to-day;
One day more bursts them open fully
    —You know the red turns grey.

To-morrow we meet the same then, dearest?
    May I take your hand in mine?
Mere friends are we,—well, friends the merest
    Keep much that I'll resign:

For each glance of that eye so bright and black,
    Though I keep with heart's endeavour,—
Your voice, when you wish the snowdrops back,
    Though it stay in my soul for ever!—

Yet I will but say what mere friends say,
    Or only a thought stronger;
I will hold your hand but as long as all may,
    Or so very little longer!

Robert Browning

TWO IN THE CAMPAGNA

I wonder do you feel today
   As I have felt since, hand in hand,
We sat down on the grass, to stray
   In spirit better through the land,
This morn of Rome and May?

For me, I touched a thought, I know,
   Has tantalized me many times,
(Like turns of thread the spiders throw
   Mocking across our path) for rhymes
To catch at and let go.

Help me to hold it! First it left
   The yellowing fennel, run to seed
There, branching from the brickwork's cleft,
   Some old tomb's ruin; yonder weed
Took up the floating weft,

Where one small orange cup amassed
   Five beetles—blind and green they grope
Among the honey-meal; and last,
   Everywhere on the grassy slope
I traced it. Hold it fast!

The champaign with its endless fleece
   Of feathery grasses everywhere!
Silence and passion, joy and peace,
   An everlasting wash of air—
Rome's ghost since her decease.

Such life here, through such length of hours,
   Such miracles performed in play,
Such primal naked forms of flowers,
   Such letting Nature have her way
While Heaven looks from its towers!

How say you? Let us, O my dove,
   Let us be unashamed of soul,
As earth lies bare to heaven above!
   How is it under our control
To love or not to love?

I would that you were all to me,
　　You that are just so much, no more,
Nor yours, nor mine, nor slave nor free!
　　Where does the fault lie? What the core
O' the wound, since wound must be?

I would I could adopt your will,
　　See with your eyes, and set my heart
Beating by yours, and drink my fill
　　At your soul's springs—your part, my part
In life, for good and ill.

No. I yearn upward—touch you close,
　　Then stand away. I kiss your cheek,
Catch your soul's warmth,—I pluck the rose
　　And love it more than tongue can speak—
Then the good minute goes.

Already how am I so far
　　Out of that minute? Must I go
Still like the thistle-ball, no bar,
　　Onward, whenever light winds blow,
Fixed by no friendly star?

Just when I seemed about to learn!
　　Where is the thread now? Off again!
The old trick! Only I discern
　　Infinite passion and the pain
Of finite hearts that yearn.

　　　　　　　　　　Robert Browning

MEETING AT NIGHT

The grey sea and the long black land;
And the yellow half-moon large and low;
And the startled little waves that leap
In fiery ringlets from their sleep,
As I gain the cove with pushing prow,
And quench its speed i' the slushy sand.

Then a mile of warm sea-scented beach;
Three fields to cross till a farm appears;
A tap at the pane, the quick sharp scratch
And blue spurt of a lighted match,
And a voice less loud, through its joys and fears,
Than the two hearts beating each to each!

Robert Browning

PORPHYRIA'S LOVER

The rain set early in tonight,
    The sullen wind was soon awake,
It tore the elm-tops down for spite,
    And did its worst to vex the lake.
    I listened with heart fit to break.
When glided in Porphyria; straight
    She shut the cold out and the storm,
And kneeled and made the cheerless grate
    Blaze up, and all the cottage warm;
    Which done, she rose, and from her form
Withdrew the dripping cloak and shawl,
    And laid her soiled gloves by, untied
Her hat and let the damp hair fall,
    And, last, she sat down by my side
    And called me. When no voice replied,
She put my arm about her waist,
    And made her smooth white shoulder bare,
And all her yellow hair displaced,
    And, stooping, made my cheek lie there,
    And spread, o'er all, her yellow hair,
Murmuring how she loved me—she
    Too weak, for all her heart's endeavor,
To set its struggling passion free
    From pride, and vainer ties dissever,
    And give herself to me for ever.
But passion sometimes would prevail,
    Nor could tonight's gay feast restrain
A sudden thought of one so pale
    For love of her, and all in vain:
    So, she was come through wind and rain.

Be sure I looked up at her eyes
  Happy and proud; at last I knew
Porphyria worshiped me; surprise
  Made my heart swell, and still it grew
  While I debated what to do.
That moment she was mine, mine, fair,
  Perfectly pure and good: I found
A thing to do, and all her hair
  In one long yellow string I wound
  Three times her little throat around,
And strangled her. No pain felt she;
  I am quite sure she felt no pain.
As a shut bud that holds a bee,
  I warily oped her lids: again
  Laughed the blue eyes without a stain.
And I untightened next the tress
  About her neck; her cheek once more
Blushed bright beneath my burning kiss:
  I propped her head up as before,
  Only, this time my shoulder bore
Her head, which droops upon it still:
  The smiling rosy little head,
So glad it has its utmost will,
  That all it scorned at once is fled,
  And I, its love, am gained instead!
Porphyria's love: she guessed not how
  Her darling one wish would be heard.
And thus we sit together now,
  And all night long we have not stirred,
  And yet God has not said a word!

                    Robert Browning

Robert Browning was in an unusually merry mood when he wrote "Muckle-Mouth Meg," a light set of verses with a surprise ending. The incident actually happened. Sir Walter Scott told the story of a young adventurer belonging to a distinguished Border tribe who was captured and doomed to be hanged. However, the wife of the victorious captor persuaded her husband to make the young gallant marry their unattractive "muckle-mouth" daughter instead. What ensued is told by Browning in a playfully dramatic manner.

MUCKLE-MOUTH MEG

Frowned the Laird, on the Lord: "So, redhanded I catch thee?
   Death-doomed by our Law of the Border!
We've a gallows outside and a chiel to dispatch thee:
   Who trespasses—hangs: all's in order."

He met frown with smile, did the young English gallant:
   Then the Laird's dame: "Nay, Husband, I beg!
He's comely: be merciful! Grace for the callant[1]
   —If he marries our Muckle-mouth Meg!"

"No mile-wide-mouthed monster of yours do I marry:
   Grant rather the gallows!" laughed he.
"Foul fare kith and kin of you—why do you tarry?"
   "To tame your fierce temper!" quoth she.

"Shove him quick in the Hole, shut him fast for a week.
   Cold, darkness, and hunger work wonders:
Who lion-like roars now, mouse-fashion will squeak,
   And 'it rains' soon succeed to 'it thunders.'"

A week did he bide in the cold and the dark
   —Not hunger: for duly at morning
In flitted a lass, and a voice like a lark
   Chirped, "Muckle-mouth Meg still ye're scorning?

"Go hang, but here's parritch[2] to hearten ye first!"
   "Did Meg's muckle-mouth boast within some
Such music as yours, mine should match it or burst:
   No frog-jaws! So tell folk, my Winsome!"

Soon week came to end, and, from Hole's door set wide,
   Out he marched, and there waited the lassie:
"Yon gallows, or Muckle-mouth Meg for a bride!
   Consider! Sky's blue and turf's grassy:

"Life's sweet: shall I say ye wed Muckle-mouth Meg?"
   "Not I," quoth the stout heart: "too eerie
The mouth that can swallow a bubblyjock's egg;
   Shall I let it munch mine? Never, Dearie!

[1] Callant: young fellow.
[2] Parritch: porridge.

"Not Muckle-mouth Meg? Wow, the obstinate man!
    Perhaps he would rather wed me!"
"Ay, would he—with just for a dowry your can!"
    "I'm Muckle-mouth Meg," chirruped she.

"Then so—so—so—so—" as he kissed her apace—
    "Will I widen thee out till thou turnest
From Margaret Minnikin-mou', by God's grace,
    To Muckle-mouth Meg in good earnest!"

Robert Browning

IS MY TEAM PLOUGHING?

"Is my team ploughing,
    That I used to drive
And hear the harness jingle
    When I was man alive?"

Aye, the horses trample,
    The harness jingles now;
No change though you lie under
    The land you used to plough.

"Is football playing
    Along the river shore,
With lads to chase the leather,
    Now I stand up no more?"

Aye, the ball is flying,
    The lads play heart and soul;
The goal stands up, the keeper
    Stands up to keep the goal.

"Is my girl happy,
    That I thought hard to leave,
And has she tired of weeping
    As she lies down at eve?"

Aye, she lies down lightly,
    She lies not down to weep:
Your girl is well contented.
    Be still, my lad, and sleep.

"Is my friend hearty,
    Now I am thin and pine;
And has he found to sleep in
    A better bed than mine?"

Aye, lad, I lie easy,
    I lie as lads would choose;
I cheer a dead man's sweetheart.
    Never ask me whose.

                    A. E. Housman

DOVER BEACH

The sea is calm tonight,
The tide is full, the moon lies fair
Upon the straits;—on the French coast the light
Gleams and is gone; the cliffs of England stand,
Glimmering and vast, out in the tranquil bay.
Come to the window, sweet is the night-air!

Only, from the long line of spray
Where the sea meets the moon-blanched land,
Listen! you hear the grating roar
Of pebbles which the waves draw back, and fling,
At their return, up the high strand,
Begin, and cease, and then again begin,
With tremulous cadence slow, and bring
The eternal note of sadness in.

Sophocles long ago
Heard it on the Aegean, and it brought
Into his mind the turbid ebb and flow
Of human misery; we
Find also in the sound a thought,
Hearing it by this distant northern sea.

The Sea of Faith
Was once, too, at the full, and round earth's shore
Lay like the folds of a bright girdle furled.
But now I only hear
Its melancholy, long, withdrawing roar,
Retreating, to the breath
Of the night-wind, down the vast edges drear
And naked shingles of the world.

Ah, love, let us be true
To one another! for the world, which seems
To lie before us like a land of dreams,
So various, so beautiful, so new,
Hath really neither joy, nor love, nor light.
Nor certitude, nor peace, nor help for pain;
And we are here as on a darkling plain
Swept with confused alarms of struggle and flight,
Where ignorant armies clash by night.

                              Matthew Arnold

THE TRUE LOVER

The lad came to the door at night,
    When lovers crown their vows,
And whistled soft and out of sight
    In shadow of the boughs.

"I shall not vex you with my face
    Henceforth, my love, for aye;
So take me in your arms a space
    Before the east is grey.

"When I from hence away am past
    I shall not find a bride,
And you shall be the first and last
    I ever lay beside."

She heard and went and knew not why;
    Her heart to his she laid;
Light was the air beneath the sky
    But dark under the shade.

"Oh do you breathe, lad, that your breast
    Seems not to rise and fall,
And here upon my bosom prest
    There beats no heart at all?"

"Oh loud, my girl, it once would knock,
    You should have felt it then;
But since for you I stopped the clock
    It never goes again."

"Oh lad, what is it, lad, that drips
    Wet from your neck on mine?
What is it falling on my lips,
    My lad, that tastes of brine?"

"Oh, like enough 'tis blood, my dear,
    For when the knife has slit
The throat across from ear to ear
    'Twill bleed because of it."

Under the stars the air was light
    But dark below the boughs,
The still air of the speechless night
    When lovers crown their vows.

A. E. Housman

In "Love on the Farm" D. H. Lawrence packs a whole vivid drama
of love and rural life in a typically Lawrentian poem intensified by "the
hot blood's blindfold art."

LOVE ON THE FARM

What large, dark hands are those at the window
Grasping in the golden light
Which weaves its way through the evening wind
    At my heart's delight?

Ah, only the leaves! But in the west
I see a redness suddenly come
Into the evening's anxious breast—
    'Tis the wound of love goes home!

The woodbine creeps abroad
Calling low to her lover:
  The sun-lit flirt who all the day
  Has poised above her lips in play
  And stolen kisses, shallow and gay
  Of pollen, now has gone away—
    She woos the moth with her sweet, low word;
And when above her his moth-wings hover
Then her bright breast she will uncover
And yield her honey-drop to her lover.

Into the yellow, evening glow
Saunters a man from the farm below;
Leans, and looks in at the low-built shed
Where the swallow has hung her marriage bed.
  The bird lies warm against the wall.
  She glances quick her startled eyes
  Towards him, then she turns away
  Her small head, making warm display
  Of red upon the throat. Her terrors sway
  Her out of the nest's warm, busy ball,
  Whose plaintive cry is heard as she flies
  In one blue stoop from out the sties
  Into the twilight's empty hall.

Oh, water-hen, beside the rushes,
Hide your quaintly scarlet blushes,
Still your quick tail, lie still as dead,
Till the distance folds over his ominous tread!

The rabbit presses back her ears,
Turns back her liquid, anguished eyes
And crouches low; then with wild spring
Spurts from the terror of his oncoming;
To be choked back, the wire ring
Her frantic effort throttling:
  Piteous brown ball of quivering fears!
Ah, soon in his large, hard hands she dies,
And swings all loose from the swing of his walk!
Yet calm and kindly are his eyes
And ready to open in brown surprise
Should I not answer to his talk
Or should he my tears surmise.

I hear his hand on the latch, and rise from my chair
Watching the door open; he flashes bare
His strong teeth in a smile, and flashes his eyes
In a smile like triumph upon me; then careless-wise
He flings the rabbit soft on the table board
And comes toward me: ah! the uplifted sword
Of his hand against my bosom! and oh, the broad
Blade of his glance that asks me to applaud
His coming! With his hand he turns my face to him
And caresses me with his fingers that still smell grim
Of rabbit's fur! God, I am caught in a snare!
I know not what fine wire is round my throat;
I only know I let him finger there
My pulse of life, and let him nose like a stoat
Who sniffs with joy before he drinks the blood.

And down his mouth comes to my mouth! and down
His bright dark eyes come over me, like a hood
Upon my mind! his lips meet mine, and a flood
Of sweet fire sweeps across me, so I drown
Against him, die, and find death good.

D. H. Lawrence

THE FIRED POT

In our town, people live in rows.
The only irregular thing in a street is the steeple:
And where that points to, God only knows,
And not the poor disciplined people!

And I have watched the women growing old,
Passionate about pins, and pence, and soap,
Till the heart within my wedded breast grew cold,
And I lost hope.

But a young soldier came to our town,
He spoke his mind most candidly.
He asked me quickly to lie down,
And that was very good for me.

For though I gave him no embrace—
Remembering my duty—
He altered the expression of my face,
And gave me back my beauty.

Anna Wickham

Best of the Australian poets, A. D. Hope waited until he was almost fifty before publishing his first volume. Not since Pope had couplets been written so deftly and divertingly as Hope's; not since Swift had satire been more devastating. Using traditional forms, Hope intensifies them with strange but exact images, stripped passion and power. "Imperial Adam" is a poem which is both witty and erotic. It begins with innocence, blossoms into pure sensuality, and ends with a shock of horror.

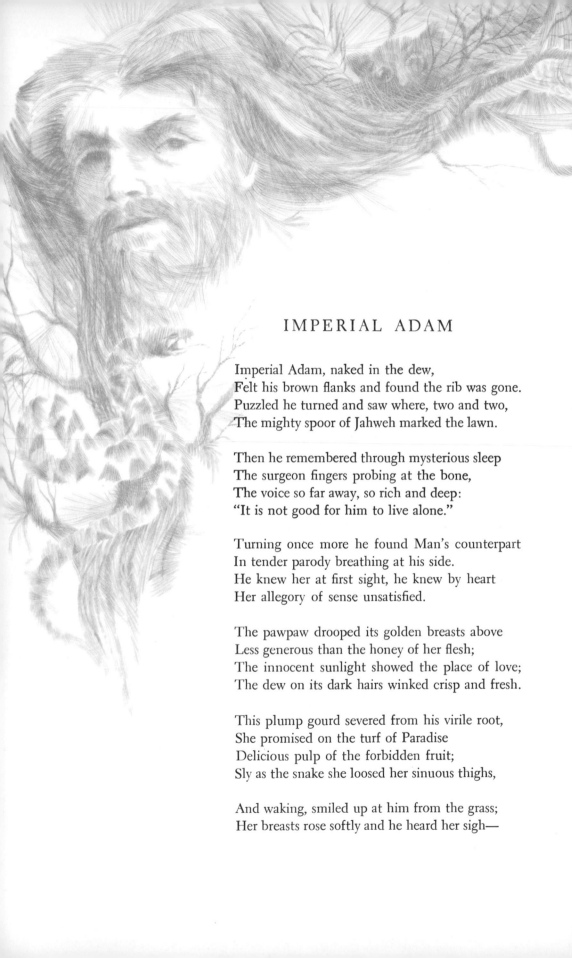

IMPERIAL ADAM

Imperial Adam, naked in the dew,
Felt his brown flanks and found the rib was gone.
Puzzled he turned and saw where, two and two,
The mighty spoor of Jahweh marked the lawn.

Then he remembered through mysterious sleep
The surgeon fingers probing at the bone,
The voice so far away, so rich and deep:
"It is not good for him to live alone."

Turning once more he found Man's counterpart
In tender parody breathing at his side.
He knew her at first sight, he knew by heart
Her allegory of sense unsatisfied.

The pawpaw drooped its golden breasts above
Less generous than the honey of her flesh;
The innocent sunlight showed the place of love;
The dew on its dark hairs winked crisp and fresh.

This plump gourd severed from his virile root,
She promised on the turf of Paradise
Delicious pulp of the forbidden fruit;
Sly as the snake she loosed her sinuous thighs,

And waking, smiled up at him from the grass;
Her breasts rose softly and he heard her sigh—

From all the beasts whose pleasant task it was
In Eden to increase and multiply

Adam had learned the jolly deed of kind:
He took her in his arms and there and then,
Like the clean beasts, embracing from behind,
Began in joy to found the breed of men.

Then from the spurt of seed within her broke
Her terrible and triumphant female cry,
Split upward by the sexual lightning stroke.
It was the beasts now who stood watching by:

The gravid elephant, the calving hind,
The breeding bitch, the she-ape big with young
Were the first gentle midwives of mankind;
The teeming lioness rasped her with her tongue;

The proud vicuña nuzzled her as she slept
Lax on the grass; and Adam watching too
Saw how her dumb breasts at their ripening wept,
The great pod of her belly swelled and grew,

And saw its water break, and saw, in fear,
Its quaking muscles in the act of birth,
Between her legs a pigmy face appear,
And the first murderer lay upon the earth.

A. D. Hope

127

The
Fulfillment
of
Love

In the Epistle of Paul to the Romans we are told to love one another, "for he that loveth hath fulfilled the law." According to Matthew Arnold "all things seek to fulfill the law of their being," and the law is love. It is a law which is also a paradox, for love takes two separate individuals and unites them in a single consciousness. "Two figures on one coin / So do they join," writes William Cavendish. Fervent protestations are innumerable, yet there are none more eloquent than the simple "I am yours; you are mine," which has been echoed and elaborated by every amorist. John Wilmot, Earl of Rochester, put aside his scandalous verse to declare:

> My light thou art. Without thy glorious sight
> My eyes are darkened with eternal night;
> My love, thou art, my way, my life, my light!

Richard Lovelace assured all lovers that stone walls do not make a prison nor iron bars a cage as long as there is fulfillment and freedom in love. Christina Rossetti sang that her heart was like a singing bird because the birthday of her life had come with the coming of love. And Sir John Suckling dismissed the doubts which vex so many lovers:

> Then farewell care, and farewell woe,
> I will no longer pine;
> For I'll believe I have her heart
> As long as she has mine.

LOVE'S CONSTANCY

> The moon shall be a darkness,
>   The stars shall give no light,
> If ever I prove false
>   To my heart's delight.
>
> In the middle of the ocean
>   Shall grow the myrtle tree,
> If ever I prove false
>   To my love who loves me.

> *Anonymous*

YOU

Seeing you smile, the furies fail to stay angry.
Watching you walk, the beggars forget they are hungry.
Yours is the breath that sets every new leaf aquiver.
Yours is the grace that guides the rush of the river.
Yours is the flush and the flame in the heart of the flower:
Life's meaning, its music, its pride and its power.

Anonymous

Guttersnipe, gangster, leader of a ring of counterfeiters and other criminals, François Villon left a collection of poems so popular that thirty-four editions of his works were issued within eighty years after his death. Villon took the outworn medieval forms and, using the language as well as the street jargon of his day, turned them into realistic ballades and roundels. Like Chaucer, he pictured himself and his times in sometimes bitter, sometimes humorous, sometimes amorous, and always penetrating poetry.

BALLADE OF THE WOMEN OF PARIS

Albeit the Venice girls get praise
  For their sweet speech and tender air,
And though the old women have wise ways
  Of chaffering for amorous ware,
  Yet at my peril dare I swear,
Search Rome, where God's grace mainly tarries,
  Florence and Savoy, everywhere,
There's no good girl's lip out of Paris.

The Naples women, as folk prattle,
  Are sweetly spoken and subtle enough:
German girls are good at tattle,
  And Prussians make their boast thereof;
  Take Egypt for the next remove,
Or that waste land the Tartar harries,
  Spain or Greece, for the matter of love,
There's no good girl's lip out of Paris.

Breton and Swiss know nought of the matter,
　　Gascony girls or girls of Toulouse;
Two fishwomen with a half-hour's chatter
　　Would shut them up by threes and twos;
Calais, Lorraine, and all their crews,
(Names enow the mad song marries)
　　England and Picardy, search them and choose,
There's no good girl's lip out of Paris.

Prince, give praise to our French ladies
　　For the sweet sound their speaking carries;
'Twixt Rome and Cadiz many a maid is,
　　But no good girl's lip out of Paris.

François Villon
translated by Algernon Charles Swinburne

BALLADE FOR A BRIDEGROOM

At day break, when the falcon claps his wings,
　　No whit for grief, but noble heart and high,
With loud glad noise he stirs himself and springs,
　　And takes his meat and toward his lure draws nigh;
　　Such good I wish you! Yea, and heartily
I am fired with hope of true love's meed to get;
　　Know that Love writes it in his book; for why,
This is the end for which we twain are met.

Mine own heart's lady with no gainsayings
　　You shall be always wholly till I die;
And in my right against all bitter things
　　Sweet laurel with fresh rose its force shall try;
　　Seeing reason wills not that I cast love by
(Nor here with reason shall I chide or fret)
　　Nor cease to serve, but serve more constantly;
This is the end for which we twain are met.

And, which is more, when grief about me clings
　　Through Fortune's fit or fume of jealousy,
Your sweet kind eye beats down her threatenings
　　As wind doth smoke; such power sits in your eye.

Thus in your field my seed of harvestry
Thrives, for the fruit is like me that I set;
   God bids me tend it with good husbandry;
This is the end for which we twain are met.

Princess, give ear to this my summary;
   That heart of mine your heart's love should forget,
Shall never be: like trust in you put I:
   This is the end for which we twain are met.

François Villon
translated by Algernon Charles Swinburne

Sidney was in love with the theme "I am yours; you are mine." Simple as a folk-tune, he used it twice: once as a sonnet, and once as the swift and artless song which follows.

MY TRUE-LOVE HATH MY HEART

My true-love hath my heart, and I have his,
By just exchange one for another given:
I hold his dear, and mine he cannot miss,
There never was a better bargain driven:
My true-love hath my heart, and I have his.

His heart in me keeps him and me in one,
My heart in him his thoughts and senses guides:
He loves my heart, for once it was his own,
I cherish his because in me it bides:
My true-love hath my heart, and I have his.

Sir Philip Sidney

SEND BACK MY HEART

I prythee send me back my heart,
Since I can not have thine:
For if from yours you will not part,
Why then should'st thou have mine?

Yet now I think on't, let it lie;
To find it were in vain,
For thou'st a thief in either eye
Would steal it back again.

Why should two hearts in one breast lie,
And yet not lodge together?
Oh Love! where is thy sympathy,
If thus our breasts thou sever?

But love is such a mystery,
I cannot find it out:
For when I think I'm best resolved,
I then am in most doubt.

Then farewell care, and farewell woe,
I will no longer pine;
For I'll believe I have her heart
As long as she has mine.

Sir John Suckling

TO ALTHEA FROM PRISON

When Love with unconfinéd wings
    Hovers within my gates,
And my divine Althea brings
    To whisper at the grates;
When I lie tangled in her hair
    And fetter'd to her eye,
The birds that wanton in the air
    Know no such liberty.

When flowing cups run swifty round
    With no allaying Thames,
Our careless heads with roses crown'd,
    Our hearts with loyal flames;
When thirsty grief in wine we steep,
    When healths and draughts go free,
Fishes that tipple in the deep
    Know no such liberty.

When, like committed linnets, I
    With shriller voice shall sing
The sweetness, mercy, majesty
    And glories of my King;
When I shall voice aloud, how good
    He is, how great should be,
Enlargéd winds that curl the flood
    Know no such liberty.

Stone walls do not a prison make,
    Nor iron bars a cage;
Minds innocent and quiet take
    That for an hermitage;
If I have freedom in my love
    And in my soul am free,
Angels alone, that soar above,
    Enjoy such liberty.

                              Richard Lovelace

The profligate John Wilmot, Earl of Rochester, wrote some of the naughtiest stanzas of the seventeenth century and some of the neatest. In the dissolute man there was a serious poet struggling to free himself from the salacious and scurrilous verse which had become his specialty.

MY LIGHT THOU ART

My light thou art. Without thy glorious sight
My eyes are darkened with eternal night;
My love, thou art my way, my life, my light.

Thou art my way; I wander if thou fly;
Thou art my light; if hid, how blind am I!
Thou art my life; if thou withdraw'st I die.

Thou art my life; if thou but turn away
My life's a thousand deaths. Thou art my way;
Without thee, love, I travel not, but stay.

                    John Wilmot, Earl of Rochester

Sir Charles Sedley belonged to the same dissipated circle that welcomed the Earl of Rochester. His only child, Catherine, inherited her father's talent for profligacy, grew up to be the mistress of James II and, as a consequence, became the Countess of Dorchester.

MY HEART AT REST

Not, Celia, that I juster am
   Or better than the rest;
For I would change each hour like them
   Were not my heart at rest.

But I am tied to very thee
   By every thought I have;
Thy face I only care to see,
   Thy heart I only crave.

All that in woman is adored
   In thy dear self I find;
For the whole sex can but afford
   The handsome and the kind.

Why then should I seek farther store,
   And still make love anew?
When change itself can give no more
   'Tis easy to be true.

                          Sir Charles Sedley

Unlike his cynical contemporaries, William Cavendish was a true lover as well as a loving husband. He did not disdain to praise fidelity and the union of two "sealed with one will."

FULFILLMENT

There is no happier life
   But in a wife;
The comforts are so sweet
   When two do meet.
'Tis plenty, peace, a calm
   Like dropping balm;
Love's weather is so fair,
   Like perfumed air.

Each word such pleasure brings
　　Like soft-touched strings;
Love's passion moves the heart
　　On either part;
Such harmony together,
　　So pleased in either.
No discords; concords still;
　　Sealed with one will.
By love, God made man one,
　　Yet not alone.
Like stamps of king and queen
　　It may be seen:
Two figures on one coin,
　　So do they join,
Only they not embrace.
　　We, face to face.

William Cavendish

I SHALL HAVE HAD MY DAY

O, let the solid ground,
   Not fail beneath my feet
Before my life has found
   What some have found so sweet;
Then let come what come may,
What matter if I go mad,
I shall have had my day.

Let the sweet heavens endure,
   Not close and darken above me
Before I am quite quite sure
   That there is one to love me!
Then let come what come may
To a life that has been so sad,
I shall have had my day.

Alfred, Lord Tennyson

Christina Rossetti was one of the most restrained and most religious of poets. Her poems of love are usually clouded with pain, resignation, and withdrawal. "I have seen her sitting in the midst of a noisy drawing room," wrote the critic Edmund Gosse, "a Sibyl whom no one had the audacity to approach." Once in a great while, however, a burst of exultation overcame her reticence. "A Birthday" is one of those rare occasions.

A BIRTHDAY

My heart is like a singing bird
   Whose nest is in a watered shoot;
My heart is like an apple-tree
   Whose boughs are bent with thick-set fruit;
My heart is like a rainbow shell
   That paddles in a halcyon sea;
My heart is gladder than all these
   Because my love is come to me.

Raise me a dais of silk and down;
  Hang it with vair[1] and purple dyes;
Carve it in doves and pomegranates,
  And peacocks with a hundred eyes;
Work it in gold and silver grapes,
  In leaves and silver fleur-de-lys;
Because the birthday of my life
  Is come, my love is come to me.

Christina Rossetti

Most flamboyant of the self-styled Pre-Raphaelite Brotherhood, Dante Gabriel Rossetti was both painter and poet. He combined the two talents in long poems that suggested the supernatural and in sonnets, such as "Silent Noon," that made silence not only visible but audible.

SILENT NOON

Your hands lie open in the long fresh grass,
The finger-points look through the rosy blooms.
Your eyes smile peace. The pasture gleams and glooms
'Neath billowing skies that scatter and amass.
All round our nest, far as the eye can pass,
Are golden kingcup-fields with silver edge
Where the cow-parsley skirts the hawthorn hedge.
'Tis visible silence, still as the hour-glass.

Deep in the sun-searched growths the dragon-fly
Hangs like a blue thread loosened from the sky:
So this winged hour is dropped to us from above.
Oh, clasp we to our hearts, for deathless dower,
This close-companioned inarticulate hour
When twofold silence was the song of love.

Dante Gabriel Rossetti

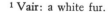

[1] Vair: a white fur.

Dante Gabriel Rossetti considered "Renouncement" one of the finest love sonnets in the language. It is a kind of companion to Christina Rossetti's "A Birthday."

RENOUNCEMENT

I must not think of thee; and tired yet strong
I shun the love that lurks in all delight—
The love of thee, and in the blue heaven's height,
And in the dearest passage of a song.
Oh, just beyond the sweetest thoughts that throng
This breast, the thought of thee waits hidden yet bright;
But it must never, never come in sight:
I must stop short of thee the whole day long.

But when sleep comes to close each difficult day,
When night gives pause to the long watch I keep,
And all my bonds I needs must loose apart,
Must doff my will as raiment laid away—
With the first dream that comes with the first sleep
I run, I run, I am gathered to thy heart!

Alice Meynell

Because of A Child's Garden of Verses, Robert Louis Stevenson is chiefly known as childhood's laureate. But Stevenson wrote not only for the very young but for the very romantic. The best of his fictional thrillers (Treasure Island and Kidnapped) and the best of his nostalgic poetry prove it.

ROMANCE

I will make you brooches and toys for your delight
Of bird-song at morning and star-shine at night.
I will make a palace fit for you and me,
Of green days in forests and blue days at sea.

I will make my kitchen, and you shall keep your room,
Where white flows the river and bright blows the broom,
And you shall wash your linen and keep your body white
In rainfall at morning and dewfall at night.

And this shall be for music when no one else is near,
The fine song for singing, the rare song to hear!
That only I remember, that only you admire,
Of the broad road that stretches and the roadside fire.

Robert Louis Stevenson

THE DARK CHAMBER

The brain forgets but the blood will remember.
  There, when the play of sense is over,
The last, low spark in the darkest chamber
  Will hold all there is of love and lover.

The war of words, the life-long quarrel
  Of self against self will resolve into nothing;
Less than the chain of berry-red coral
  Crying against the dead black of her clothing.

What has the brain that it hopes to last longer?
  The blood will take from forgotten violence
The groping, the break of her voice in anger.
  There will be left only music and silence.

These will remain, these will go searching
  Your veins for life when the flame of life smolders:
The night that you two saw the mountains marching
  Up against dawn with the stars on their shoulders;

The jetting poplars' arrested fountains
  As you drew her under them, easing her pain;
The notes, not the words, of a half-finished sentence.
  The music, the silence. . . . These will remain.

Louis Untermeyer

TO A WEEPING WILLOW

You hypocrite!
You sly deceiver!
I have watched you fold your hands and sit
With your head bowed the slightest bit,
And your body bending and swaying
As though you were praying,
Like a devout and rapt believer.
You knew that folks were looking and you were
Well pleased with the effect of it:
Your over-mournful mien;
Your meek and almost languid stir;
Your widow's weeds of trailing green.
Wearing a grief in resignation clad,
You seemed so chastely, delicately sad.

You bold, young hypocrite—
I know you now!
Last night when every light was out,
I saw you wave one beckoning bough
And, with a swift and passionate shout,
The storm sprang up—and you, you exquisite,
You laughed a welcome to that savage lout.
I heard that thunder of his heavy boots.
And then in that dark, rushing weather,
You clung together;
Safe with your secret in the night's great cover,
You and your lover.
I saw his windy fingers in your hair;
I saw you tremble and try to tear
Free from your roots
In a headlong rush to him.
His face was dim.
But I could hear his kisses in the rain,
And I could see your arms clasp and unclasp.
His rough, impetuous grasp
Shook you and you let fall
Your torn and futile weeds; then flung them all
Joyfully in the air,
As though they were
Triumphant flags, to sing above
The stark and shameless victory of love!

Louis Untermeyer

SINCE I SAW MY LOVE

I was so chill, and overworn, and sad,
To be a lady was the only joy I had.
I walked the street as silent as a mouse,
Buying fine clothes, and fittings for the house.

But since I saw my love
I wear a simple dress,
And happily I move
Forgetting weariness.

Anna Wickham

THE MAN WITH A HAMMER

My Dear was a mason
    And I was his stone;
And quick did he fashion
    A house of his own.

As fish in the waters,
    As birds in the tree,
So natural and blithe lives
    His spirit in me.

Anna Wickham

*In one of his sonnets Shakespeare promises immortality to his love.
It begins:*

Not marble, nor the gilded monuments
Of princes, shall outlive this powerful rhyme.

*"Your praise," it continues, "shall still find room even in the eyes of
all posterity," and it ends:*

So, till the judgment that yourself arise,
You live in this, and dwell in lovers' eyes.

*Borrowing Shakespeare's line for his title, Archibald MacLeish seems
less boastful but is no less impassioned about the poet's power to im-
mortalize his beloved.*

142

"NOT MARBLE, NOR THE GILDED MONUMENTS"

The praisers of women in their proud and beautiful poems,
Naming the grave mouth and the hair and the eyes,
Boasted those they loved should be forever remembered:
These were lies.

The words sound but the face in the Istrian sun is forgotten.
The poet speaks, but to her dead ears no more.
The sleek throat is gone—and the breast that was troubled to listen:
Shadow from door.

Therefore I will not praise your knees nor your fine walking,
Telling you men shall remember your name as long
As lips move or breath is spent or the iron of English
Rings from a tongue.

I shall say you were young and your arms straight, and your mouth
    scarlet:
I shall say you will die and none will remember you:
Your arms change, and none remember the swish of your garments,
Nor the click of your shoe.

Not with my hand's strength, not with difficult labor
Springing the obstinate words to the bones of your breast
And the stubborn line to your young stride and the breath to your breath-
    ing
And the beat to your haste
Shall I prevail on the hearts of unborn men to remember.

(What is a dead girl but a shadowy ghost
Or a dead man's voice but a distant and vain affirmation
Like dream words most)

Therefore I will not speak of the undying glory of women.
I will say you were young and straight and your skin fair
And you stood in the door and the sun was a shadow of leaves on your
    shoulders
And a leaf on your hair—

I will not speak of the famous beauty of dead women:
I will say the shape of a leaf lay once on your hair.
Till the world ends and the eyes are out and the mouths broken
Look! It is there!

Archibald MacLeish

In White-Haired Lover *Karl Shapiro wrote of a Roman poet who, at the age of fifty-odd, fell violently and reluctantly in love. Karl Shapiro was also fifty-odd when his cycle of twenty-nine love poems was published. The experimental poet returned to the traditional manner that he had abandoned and, for good measure, added a fairly strictly patterned, old-fashioned favorite French form.*

BALLADE

Here ends this cycle of my poems for you
Since we have passed from poetry into life,
You give me everything that love can do,
I think you say you want to be my wife,
Yet some suspicion pricks me like a knife
As if some guilty party, you or I,
Shadows our love with doubt and disbelief
That you will not be with me till I die.

Or bastard that I am and poet and Jew
As you grow quiet and strong I cause you grief,
Fighting what I desire, the group of two,
And thieve your beauty like a sickly thief,
Possessing you in phantasy—in brief
Betraying all this joy for poetry,
So terrified our love will not be safe,
That you will not be with me till I die.

My heart knows none of this is really true,
The fear, the guilt, the business of the grave.
What haven't you given, what haven't you made new
And strong and beautiful in this twilight cave?
You give me everything that love can crave,
You give me everything that love can try,
You even liberate me as love's slave:
"That you will not be with me till I die."

Dear love, our love is only what we gave
And what awaits, whether we laugh or cry;
God strike me if I question what we have
And that you'll not be with me till I die.

Karl Shapiro

WINTER TRYST

Love's delight
On a frosty night
Shines brighter for
The dark trees whispering
Sedition around the house
And the fire within.

Open the door to the wind:
The word sin
Is a delicious tempter
As the cat steps in
With his lopsided grin.

He knows we know
He knows. His yellow eyes
Glow. He's wise. So,
While the winds blow,

Now comes the hour
In which we must devour
Us, time, and light.
Out, night.
       In, cat. Don't go.
We need you here, for though

We, in heedless flight,
Blow out each spark
Along love's leaping arc
Of fire, and all is dark
To sight, your eyes will light
Our way home through the night.

Ormonde de Kay, Jr.

145

"All the Tree's Hands" is not so much a recall of passion as a remembered response to its aftermath. The gentle, sliding cadences express a sensibility that is personal in utterance and universal in application.

ALL THE TREE'S HANDS

All the tree's hands
hung empty
> of dark and rain

and we stood beneath them
breathing twilight as a smoke
never touching
> nor looking anywhere but up.

We cried for those high hung hands
to touch us, a blessing or laying on of,
some touch we had not owned.
> The hands
hung high and empty of us, making no sign
or gesture,
> leaving us to love
and that gentleness
> after
> > among trees.

Jeannette Nichols

146

Born in London, daughter of a Russian Jew who became an Anglican clergyman and married a Welsh woman, Denise Levertov was brought up on the Bible, Jewish jokes, and Welsh folklore. Her first poems were printed when she was sixteen. Since then, married to an American writer, Mitchell Goodman, she has published half a dozen volumes of disciplined nervous perceptions distinguished by a delicate feminine awareness.

THE WIFE

A frog under you,
knees drawn up
ready to leap out of time,

a dog beside you,
snuffing at you, seeking
scent of you, an idea unformulated,

I give up on
trying to answer my question,
Do I love you enough?

It's enough to be
so much here. And
certainly when I catch

your mind in the
act of plucking
truthfromthedarksurroundingnowhere

as a swallow skims a
gnat from the
deep sky,

I don't stop to ask myself
Do I love him? but
laugh for joy.

Denise Levertov

Scholar, teacher, and author of a sober study of world population growth, Philip Appleman is also a poet. Summer Love and Surf opens with "Crystal Anniversary," a simple tribute to marriage accomplished with subtle grace and a tour de force of suspended or oblique rhymes.

CRYSTAL ANNIVERSARY

Deep in a glassy ball, the future looks
Impacted, overdue, a thing that ticks
And dings with promise, but will not happen; we,
Meanwhile, tick-and-dinging through the glow
Of one more married morning, mind the clock
Of age, fading slowly into black-
On-white biographies. The crimson bird
You welcomed sunrise with, and somehow scared,
Has skirred off, blazing, to a hazy past. Still,
It's all there, deep in the glassy ball,
The past as future: you and that morning flash
Of wings bore anniversaries, a rush
Of visions—you, golden on a far-off beach
Sand-silver—anniversary of such
An earlier you, ringed with the flickering churn
Of antique fountains—anniversary again
Of you, you, dazzling in the fever of love
And smiling on those nights we'd hardly move,
But stand for hours, deep in crystal flakes
Of bundled, quiet winter, touching cheeks.
It wasn't then our worst, or yet our best:
It was the first.

Philip Appleman

Besides being a short story writer of subtle effectiveness, Nancy Cardozo is a poet. "Day Dream" from a sequence of love poems entitled "Letter from a Far Country" is, like her other work, a combination of strength and delicacy.

DAY DREAM

Horses of summer
graze in the valley.
They are shy,
they run from the bells of the bridle.

I would mount the wildest,
the fleetest,
and ride the hills of the world
till I come to you,

my thighs wet from the foaming flanks
and the early dew.

Nancy Cardozo

The
Gallantry
of
Love

There is a side of love which is too little appreciated: its gallantry. It includes not only courage but also courtesy, pride and protectiveness. It is in Edmund Spenser's tribute:

> You frame my thoughts and fashion me within;
> You stop my tongue and teach my heart to speak;
> You calm the storm that passion did begin . . .

Gallantry inspires Ben Jonson's imperishable "Drink to Me Only with Thine Eyes," Richard Lovelace's "To Lucasta, on Going to the Wars," Thomas Carew's assurance that, when he dies, the picture of his beloved will be found hidden in his heart, and Robert Burns' lyric of tender guardianship, "O Wert Thou in the Cauld Blast."

It is interesting to note that gallantry evokes little response from modern poets. There seems to be no time in this high-pressured age for old-fashioned courtesies.

MORE THAN MOST FAIR

> More than most fair, full of the living fire
> Kindled above unto the Maker near:
> No eyes, but joys, in which all powers conspire,
> That to the world naught else be counted dear:
> Through your bright beams doth not the blinded guest
> Shoot out his darts to base affection's wound;
> But angels come, to lead frail minds to rest
> In chaste desires, on heavenly beauty bound.
> You frame my thoughts and fashion me within;
> You stop my tongue and teach my heart to speak;
> You calm the storm that passion did begin;
> Strong through your cause, but by your virtue weak.
> 　Dark is the world where your light shinéd never;
> 　Well is he born that may behold you ever.

> *Edmund Spenser*

FEAR NOT, DEAR LOVE

Fear not, dear love, that I'll reveal
Those hours of pleasure we both steal;
No eye shall see, nor yet the sun
Descry what thou and I have done.

No ear shall hear our love, but we
Silent as the night will be;
The god of love himself, whose dart
Did first wound mine and then thy heart,

Shall never know, that we can tell,
What sweets in stol'n embraces dwell.
This only means may find it out,
If, when I die, physicians doubt

What caused my death, and there to view
Of all their judgments which was true,
Rip up my heart. Oh! then, I fear,
The world will see thy picture there.

Thomas Carew

DRINK TO ME ONLY WITH THINE EYES

Drink to me only with thine eyes,
    And I will pledge with mine;
Or leave a kiss but in the cup
    And I'll not look for wine.
The thirst that from the soul doth rise
    Doth ask a drink divine;
But might I of Jove's nectar sup,
    I would not change for thine.

I sent thee late a rosy wreath,
    Not so much honoring thee
As giving it a hope that there
    It could not withered be;
But thou thereon didst only breathe
    And sent'st it back to me;
Since when it grows, and smells, I swear,
    Not of itself but thee!

Ben Jonson

TO LUCASTA, ON GOING TO THE WARS

Tell me not, Sweet, I am unkind
  That from the nunnery
Of thy chaste breast and quiet mind,
  To war and arms I fly.

True, a new mistress now I chase,
  The first foe in the field;
And with a stronger faith embrace
  A sword, a horse, a shield.

Yet this inconstancy is such
  That you too shall adore;
I could not love thee, dear, so much
  Loved I not honor more.

Richard Lovelace

153

O WERT THOU IN THE CAULD BLAST

O wert thou in the cauld blast
  On yonder lea, on yonder lea,
My plaidie to the angry airt,
  I'd shelter thee, I'd shelter thee.
Or did misfortune's bitter storms
  Around thee blaw, around thee blaw,
Thy bield[1] should be my bosom,
  To share it a', to share it a'.

Or were I in the wildest waste,
  Sae black and bare, sae black and bare,
The desert were a paradise
  If thou wert there, if thou wert there.
Or were I monarch o' the globe,
  Wi' thee to reign, wi' thee to reign,
The brightest jewel in my crown
  Wad be my queen, wad be my queen.

Robert Burns

SWEET AFTON

Flow gently, sweet Afton! among thy green braes,
Flow gently, I'll sing thee a song in thy praise;
My Mary's asleep by thy murmuring stream,
Flow gently, sweet Afton, disturb not her dream.

Thou stock-dove whose echo resounds through the glen,
Ye wild whistling blackbirds in yon thorny den,
Thou green-crested lapwing, thy screaming forbear,
I charge you, disturb not my slumbering fair.

How lofty, sweet Afton, thy neighboring hills,
Far marked with the courses of clear, winding rills;
There daily I wander as noon rises high,
My flocks and my Mary's sweet cot in my eye.

[1] Bield: a haven, a protection.

How pleasant thy banks and green valleys below,
Where, wild in the woodlands, the primroses blow;
There oft, as mild ev'ning weeps over the lea,
The sweet-scented birk shades my Mary and me.

Thy crystal stream, Afton, how lovely it glides,
And winds by the cot where my Mary resides;
How wanton thy waters her snowy feet lave,
As, gathering sweet flowerets, she stems thy clear wave.

Flow gently, sweet Afton, among thy green braes,
Flow gently, sweet river, the theme of my lays;
My Mary's asleep by thy murmuring stream,
Flow gently, sweet Afton, disturb not her dream.

Robert Burns

The
Ecstasy
of
Love

For most lovers, love means rapture and restless ecstasy. There are no restraints to its transports; the expression of ecstasy is limitless. In the midst of Holy Writ, a sudden surprise between the skeptical commentary of Ecclesiastes and the prophecies of Isaiah, is the Song of Songs, one of the most burningly beautiful of all love poems.

Bliss has no borderlines. There is the wild cry of longing in "O Western Wind," perhaps the most emotion-packed four lines ever written, and there is the quiet exaltation of "There Is a Lady." There is the devotion of the entangled lover who would die in bondage rather than break one hair to gain his liberty, and there is John Donne's reproof to the unruly sun for rousing him from the bed of love that pays no heed to hours, days, or months "which are the rags of time." There is the straightforward folksong-like tune of Burns' "A Red, Red Rose," and there is Shelley's swooning and almost overwrought "Indian Serenade." There is Byron's calm eloquence—rare in that theatrical romancer—in "She Walks in Beauty," and there is Francis Thompson's exotic "Arab Love Song." Finally, a brief fourteen-line drama, there is Rupert Brooke's sonnet that begins so buoyantly:

> Breathless, we flung us on the windy hill,
> Laughed in the sun, and kissed the lovely grass. . .

and ends so poignantly:

> And then you suddenly cried, and turned away.

Here, as so often in the poetry of love, ecstasy and anxiety are intertwined.

BEHOLD, THOU ART FAIR

> Behold, thou art fair, my love;
> Behold, thou art fair;
> Thou hast doves' eyes within thy locks:
> Thy hair is as a flock of goats that appear from mount Gilead.

Thy teeth are like a flock of sheep that are even shorn,
Which came up from the washing;
Whereof every one bear twins,
And none is barren among them.
Thy lips are like a thread of scarlet,
And thy speech is comely;
Thy temples are like a piece of a pomegranate
Within thy locks;
Thy neck is like the tower of David
Builded for an armory,
Whereon there hang a thousand bucklers,
All shields of mighty men.
Thy two breasts are like two young roes that are twins,
Which feed among the lilies.

Until the day break, and the shadows flee away,
I will get me to the mountain of myrrh,
And to the hill of frankincense.

Thou art all fair, my love;
There is no spot in thee.
Come with me from Lebanon, my spouse,
With me from Lebanon:
Look from the top of Amana,
From the top of Shenir and Hermon,
From the lions' dens,
From the mountains of the leopards.
Thou hast ravished my heart, my sister, my spouse;
Thou hast ravished my heart with one of thine eyes,
With one chain of thy neck.

How fair is thy love, my sister, my spouse!
How much better is thy love than wine!
And the smell of thine ointments than all spices!
Thy lips, O my spouse, drop as the honeycomb:
Honey and milk are under thy tongue;
And the smell of thy garments is like the smell of Lebanon.

A garden inclosed in my sister, my spouse;
A spring shut up, a fountain sealed.
Thy plants are an orchard of pomegranates,
With pleasant fruits; camphire, with spikenard,
Spikenard and saffron;
Calamus and cinnamon,
With all trees of frankincense;
Myrrh and aloes.
With all the chief spices:
A fountain of gardens,
A well of living waters,
And streams from Lebanon.

Awake, O north wind, and come, thou south;
Blow upon my garden,
That the spices thereof may flow out.
Let my beloved come into his garden,
And eat his pleasant fruits.

The Song of Songs

O WESTERN WIND

O Western wind, when wilt thou blow
That the small rain down can rain?
Christ, that my love were in my arms,
And I in my bed again!

Anonymous

THERE IS A LADY

There is a lady sweet and kind,
Was never face so pleased my mind;
I did but see her passing by,
And yet I love her till I die.

Her gesture, motion, and her smiles,
Her wit, her voice my heart beguiles,
Beguiles my heart, I know not why,
And yet I love her till I die.

Cupid is wingéd and doth range
Her country so my love doth change:
But change the earth, or change the sky,
Yet will I love her till I die.

Anonymous

SO FAST ENTANGLED

Her hair the net of golden wire,
Wherein my heart, led by my wandering eyes,
So fast entangled is that in no wise
It can, nor will, again retire;
But rather will in that sweet bondage die
Than break one hair to gain its liberty.

Anonymous

THE SUN RISING

Busy old fool, unruly Sun,
    Why dost thou thus,
Through windows, and through curtains, call on us?
Must to thy motions lovers' seasons run?
    Saucy pedantic wretch, go chide
    Late school-boys and sour prentices,
Go tell court-huntsmen that the king will ride,
Call country ants to harvest offices;
Love, all alike, no season knows nor clime,
Nor hours, days, months, which are the rags of time.

Thy beams so reverend and strong
Why shouldst thou think?
I could eclipse and cloud them with a wink,
But that I would not lose her sight so long.
If her eyes have not blinded thine,
Look, and tomorrow late tell me,
Whether both th' Indias of spice and mine
Be where thou left'st them, or lie here with me.
Ask for those kings whom thou saw'st yesterday,
And thou shalt hear, "All here in one bed lay."

She's all states, and all princes I;
Nothing else is.
Princes do but play us; compared to this,
All honor's mimic, all wealth alchemy.
Thou, Sun, art half as happy as we,
In that the world's contracted thus;
Thine age asks ease, and since thy duties be
To warm the world, that's done in warming us.
Shine here to us, and thou art everywhere;
This bed thy centre is, these walls thy sphere.

John Donne

GO, LOVELY ROSE!

Go, lovely rose!
Tell her, that wastes her time and me,
That now she knows,
When I resemble her to thee,
How sweet and fair she seems to be.

Tell her that's young
And shuns to have her graces spied,
That hadst thou sprung
In deserts, where no men abide,
Thou must have uncommended died.

Small is the worth
Of beauty from the light retired:
Bid her come forth,
Suffer herself to be desired,
And not blush so to be admired.

Then die! that she
The common fate of all things rare
May read in thee:
How small a part of time they share
That are so wondrous sweet and fair!

Edmund Waller

ASK ME NO MORE

Ask me no more where Jove bestows,
When June is past, the fading rose;
For in your beauty's orient deep
These flowers, as in their causes, sleep.

Ask me no more whither do stray
The golden atoms of the day;
For in pure love heaven did prepare
Those powders to enrich your hair.

Ask me no more whither doth haste
The nightingale, when May is past;
For in your sweet dividing throat
She winters, and keeps warm her note.

Ask me no more where those stars light,
That downwards fall in dead of night;
For in your eyes they sit, and there
Fixed become, as in their sphere.

Ask me no more if east or west
The phœnix builds her spicy nest;
For unto you at last she flies,
And in your fragrant bosom dies.

Thomas Carew

ON A GIRDLE

That which her slender waist confined
Shall now my joyful temples bind;
No monarch but would give his crown
His arms might do what this has done.

It was my heaven's extremest sphere,
The pale which held that lovely deer;
My joy, my grief, my hope, my love
Did all within this circle move.

A narrow compass! and yet there
Dwelt all that's good and all that's fair.
Give me but what this ribband bound,
Take all the rest the sun goes round.

Edmund Waller

A RED, RED ROSE

O my Luve's like a red, red rose
That's newly sprung in June:
O my Luve's like the melodie
That's sweetly played in tune.

As fair art thou, my bonnie lass,
So deep in luve am I:
And I will luve thee still, my dear,
Till a' the seas gang dry.

Till a' the seas gang dry, my dear,
And the rocks melt wi' the sun:
And I will luve thee still, my dear,
While the sands o' life shall run.

And fare thee weel, my only Luve!
And fare thee weel a while!
And I will come again, my Luve,
Tho' it were ten thousand mile.

Robert Burns

TO DREAM OF THEE

(From *Lines to Fanny*)

O, for some sunny spell
To dissipate the shadows of this hell!
Say they are gone—with the new dawning light
Steps forth my lady bright!
O, let me once more rest
My soul upon that dazzling breast!
Let once again these aching arms be placed,
The tender gaolers of thy waist!
And let me feel that warm breath here and there
To spread a rapture in my very hair!
O, the sweetness of the pain!
Give me those lips again!
Enough! Enough! It is enough for me
To dream of thee!

John Keats

THE INDIAN SERENADE

I arise from dreams of thee
In the first sweet sleep of night,
When the winds are breathing low,
And the stars are shining bright:
I arise from dreams of thee,
And a spirit in my feet
Hath led me—who knows how?
To thy chamber window, Sweet!

The wandering airs they faint
On the dark, the silent stream—
The champak odors fail
Like sweet thoughts in a dream;
The nightingale's complaint,
It dies upon her heart;
As I must on thine,
Oh, beloved as thou art!

O lift me from the grass!
I die! I faint! I fail!
Let thy love in kisses rain
On my lips and eyelids pale.
My cheek is cold and white, alas!
My heart beats loud and fast;—
Oh! press it to thine own again,
Where it will break at last.

Percy Bysshe Shelley

SHE WALKS IN BEAUTY

She walks in beauty, like the night
Of cloudless climes and starry skies,
And all that's best of dark and bright
Meet in her aspect and her eyes;
Thus mellowed to that tender light
Which heaven to gaudy day denies.

One shade the more, one ray the less,
Had half impaired the nameless grace
Which waves in every raven tress
Or softly lightens o'er her face,
Where thoughts serenely sweet express
How pure, how dear their dwelling-place.

And on that cheek and o'er that brow
So soft, so calm, yet eloquent,
The smiles that win, the tints that glow
But tell of days in goodness spent,
A mind at peace with all below,
A heart whose love is innocent.

George Gordon, Lord Byron

A prime eccentric, Thomas Lovell Beddoes persuaded himself that
he was a displaced Elizabethan; he even cultivated a short beard to
look like Shakespeare. A play, The Bride's Tragedy, written at eighteen,
was hailed as a remarkable anachronism, a seventeenth-century drama
written in the nineteenth century. It started its author on a series of
morbid tragedies interspersed with sensuous and even sentimental lyrics.

HOW MANY TIMES?

How many times do I love thee, dear?
　Tell me how many thoughts there be
　　In the atmosphere
　　Of a new-fall'n year,
Whose white and sable hours appear
　The latest flake of Eternity:
So many times do I love thee, dear.

How many times do I love again?
　Tell me how many beads there are
　　In a silver chain
　　Of evening rain,
Unravelled from the tumbling main,
　And threading the eye of a yellow star:
So many times do I love again.

Thomas Lovell Beddoes

A mystic and a rhapsodist, Francis Thompson illuminated all his
poems with the same brilliant colors that characterize his extraordinary
"The Hound of Heaven." The little lyric which he called "An Arab
Love-Song" is oriental only in the richness of Thompson's images.
The very opening is a fantasy—"the hunchéd camels of the night" are
not, as the reader might at first suppose, actual objects but cloud-shapes.

167

AN ARAB LOVE-SONG

The hunchéd camels of the night
Trouble the bright
And silver waters of the moon.
The Maiden of the Morn will soon
Through Heaven stray and sing,
Star gathering.

Now while the dark about our loves is strewn,
Light of my dark, blood of my heart, O come!
And night will catch her breath up, and be dumb.

Leave thy father, leave thy mother
And thy brother;
Leave the black tents of thy tribe apart!
Am I not thy father and thy brother,
And thy mother?
And thou—what needest with thy tribe's black tents
Who hast the red pavilion of my heart?

Francis Thompson

TO HELEN

Helen, thy beauty is to me
Like those Nicaean barks of yore,
That gently, o'er a perfumed sea,
The weary, wayworn wanderer bore
To his own native shore.

On desperate seas long wont to roam,
Thy hyacinth hair, thy classic face,
Thy Naiad airs, have brought me home
To the glory that was Greece
And the grandeur that was Rome.

Lo! in yon brilliant window-niche
How statue-like I see thee stand,
The agate lamp within thy hand!
As, Psyche, from the regions which
Are Holy Land!

Edgar Allan Poe

"Who touches this book, touches a man," cried Walt Whitman. It was a justified boast. His lusty spirit shouts its way through the all-embracing Leaves of Grass. The following passage is a particularly rousing invocation from the book's central poem, "Song of Myself."

PRESS CLOSE BARE-BOSOM'D NIGHT

Press close bare-bosom'd night—press close magnetic nourishing night!
Night of south winds—night of the large few stars!
Still nodding night—mad naked summer night.

Smile O voluptuous cool-breath'd earth!
Earth of the slumbering and liquid trees!
Earth of departed sunset—earth of the mountains misty-topt!
Earth of the vitreous pour of the full moon just tinged with blue!
Earth of shine and dark mottling the tide of the river!
Earth of the limpid gray of clouds brighter and clearer for my sake!
Far-swooping elbow'd earth—rich apple-blossom'd earth!
Smile, for your lover comes.

Prodigal, you have given me love—therefore I to you give love!
O unspeakable passionate love.

Walt Whitman

Novelist, playwright, poet, polemicist, Robert Penn Warren infuses everything he touches with intensity. Fantasy and fierce commitment, violence and tenderness fluctuate through his poems which have won prizes as well as national awards. "Love: Two Vignettes" captures and communicates the physical "instant joy," the heart's wild taking-off in ecstasy.

LOVE: TWO VIGNETTES

1. Mediterranean Beach: Day After Storm

> How instant joy, how clang
> And whang the sun, how
> Whoop the sea, and oh,
> Sun, sing, as whiter than
> Rage of snow, let sea the spume
> Fling.

Let sea, the spume, white, fling,
White on blue wild
With wind, let sun
Sing, while the world
Scuds, clouds boom and belly,
Creak like sails, whiter than,
Brighter than,
Spume in sun-song, oho!
The wind is bright.

Wind the heart winds
In constant coil, turning
In the—forever—light.

Give me your hand.

2. *Deciduous Spring*

Now, now, the world
All gabblesjoy like geese, for
An idiot glory the sky
Bangs. Look!
All leaves are new, are
Now, are
Bangles dangling and
Spangling, in sudden air
Wangling, then
Hanging quiet, bright.

The world comesback, and again
Is gabbling, and yes,
Remarkably worse, for
The world is a whirl of
Green mirrors gone wild with
Deceit, and the world
Whirls green on a string, then
The leaves go quiet, wink
From their own shade, secretly.

Keep still just a moment, leaves.

There is something I am trying to remember.

Robert Penn Warren

Estimates of Rupert Brooke's poetry have changed considerably since the time when, in *1915*, his lines "If I should die, think only this of me / That there's some corner of a foreign field / That is forever England" elicited weeping when the sonnet was read not only in English schools and churches but also in Parliament. Yet, although Brooke's importance has been questioned by modern critics, in his twenty-seven years—he was an early casualty of the First World War—Brooke wrote half a dozen poems which delight in the things of this world and in the life of the mind. In a review of Brooke's Collected Poems a few years after his death, Virginia Woolf recalled "his inquisitive eagerness about life, his response to every side of it, and his complex power of testing and enjoying, of suffering and taking with the utmost sharpness the impression of everything that came his way."

THE HILL

Breathless, we flung us on the windy hill,
Laughed in the sun, and kissed the lovely grass.
You said, "Through glory and ecstasy we pass;
Wind, sun, and earth remain, the birds sing still,
When we are old, are old. . . ." "And when we die
All's over that is ours; and life burns on
Through other lovers, other lips," said I,
"Heart of my heart, our heaven is now, is won!"
"We are Earth's best, that learnt her lesson here.
Life is our cry. We have kept the faith!" we said;
"We shall go down with unreluctant tread
Rose-crowned into the darkness! . . ." Proud we were,
And laughed, that had such brave true things to say.
And then you suddenly cried, and turned away.

Rupert Brooke

The
Urgency
of
Love

"Had we but world enough, and time," Marvell complains with all a lover's eagerness and sense of time's urgency. Whitman echoes the universal insistence:

> Urge and urge and urge,
> Always the procreant urge of the world.

The demand for consummation has inspired a vast poetry of physical longing, a poetry that ranges from the delicately erotic to the frankly sensual, from the pretty paganism of Campion, Carew, and Waller, to the perverse pleasures of Swinburne and Symons.

The urgency of love also prompts a poetry in which the fulfillment is spiritual as well as physical. The poetry of passion often lifts unrestrained feeling to the pitch of supersensual transports. Desire and devotion combine in the far-reaching sonnets by Shakespeare, in the resounding lyrics by Shelley, Browning, and Tennyson, as well as in contemporary poetry. The imperative need of bodily delight and transcendental rapture may change its expression and alter its form, but it cannot lose its fervor.

FROM "THE GREEK ANTHOLOGY"

> Dawn, enemy of love, how slow you creep
> Across the sky when I am forced to sleep
> Sadly alone. But oh, how fast you fly
> When she is in my arms and night goes by.

> "Mockery murders love," they say—and she
> Laughed in my face last night and slammed her door.
> I swore to stay away from her. But see,
> It's break of day—and here I am once more!

Lifting my eyes from Hesiod's great book,
I saw young Pyrrha pass and nod,
Linger, and give another look . . .
Good-bye to dull old Hesiod.

My girl is dark, but she is my desire;
And she is mine, dark body and dark soul.
Yes, it is true, my girl is black as coal.
But what gives greater warmth than coal on fire?

Put out the light and let the embers die;
The room will not grow cold while you and I
Are clinging-close and all aglow. Indeed
Love is the only fire that lovers need.

With wine and words of love and fervent vow
   He lulled me into bed. I closed my eyes,
A sleepy, stupid innocent . . . And now
   I dedicate the spoils of my surprise:
The silk that bound my breasts, my virgin zone,
   The cherished purity I could not keep.
Venus, remember we were all alone,
   And he was strong—and I was half-asleep.

Adapted by Louis Untermeyer

One of the loveliest of English lyrics is actually of Latin origin. Thomas Campion's "My sweetest Lesbia, let us live and love" is a transcription of Catullus' Vivamus, mea Lesbia, atque amemus. A classic in two languages, it is a triumph of expression, rich and simple, and interesting to compare with Ben Jonson's paraphrase ("Come, My Celia") on page 16.

174

LET US LIVE AND LOVE

My sweetest Lesbia, let us live and love;
And though the sager sort our deeds reprove,
Let us not weigh them. Heaven's great lamps do dive
Into their west, and straight again revive;
But, soon as once set is our little light,
Then must we sleep one ever-during night.

If all would lead their lives in love like me,
Then bloody swords and armor should not be;
No drum nor trumpet peaceful sleeps should move,
Unless alarm came from the camp of love.
But fools do live and waste their little light,
And seek with pain their ever-during night.

When timely death my life and fortune ends,
Let not my hearse be vexed with mourning friends;
But let all lovers rich in triumph come,
And with sweet pastime grace my happy tomb.
And, Lesbia, close up thou my little light,
And crown with love my ever-during night.

Catullus, adapted by Thomas Campion

Besides being a poet, Campion was a composer who set his own lyrics to music. He was acclaimed in his day for his masques and marriage odes as well as hymns and funeral dirges which filled four Books of Airs. His songs have outlived most of the words and melodies of the late sixteenth and early seventeenth centuries.

MY LIFE'S DELIGHT

Come, O come, my life's delight,
  Let me not in languor pine!
Love loves no delay; thy sight,
  The more enjoyed, the more divine:
O come, and take from me
The pain of being deprived of thee!

Thou all sweetness dost enclose,
    Like a little world of bliss.
Beauty guards thy looks: the rose
    In them pure and eternal is.
Come, then, and make thy flight
And swift to me, as heavenly light.

Thomas Campion

WHEN WE COURT AND KISS

I care not for these ladies
That must be wooed and prayed;
Give me kind Amaryllis,
The wanton country maid.
Nature art disdaineth,
Her beauty is her own.
Her, when we court and kiss,
She cries, "Forsooth, let go!"
But when we come where comfort is,
She never will say no.

If I love Amaryllis,
She gives me fruit and flowers,
But if we love these ladies,
We must give golden showers.
Give them gold that sell love;
Give me the nut-brown lass,
Who, when we court and kiss,
She cries, "Forsooth, let go!"
But when we come where comfort is,
She never will say no.

These ladies must have pillows
And beds by strangers wrought;
Give me a bower of willows,
Of moss and leaves unbought,
And fresh Amaryllis
With milk and honey fed,
Who, when we court and kiss,
She cries, "Forsooth, let go!"
But when we come where comfort is,
She never will say no.

Thomas Campion

FOLLOW YOUR SAINT

Follow your saint, follow with accents sweet!
Haste you, sad notes, fall at her flying feet!
There, wrapped in clouds of sorrow, pity move,
And tell the ravisher of my soul I perish for her love.
But, if she scorns my never-ceasing pain,
Then burst with sighing in her sight, and ne'er return again.

All that I sang still to her praise did tend,
Still she was first, still she my songs did end;
Yet she my love and music both doth fly,
The music that her echo is and beauty's sympathy.
Then let my notes pursue her scornful flight!
It shall suffice that they were breathed, and died for her delight.

Thomas Campion

MORE LOVE OR MORE DISDAIN

Give me more love or more disdain;
    The torrid or the frozen zone
Bring equal ease unto my pain,
    The temperate affords me none:
Either extreme of love or hate,
Is sweeter than a calm estate.

Give me a storm; if it be love,
    Like Danaë in that golden shower,
I swim in pleasure; if it prove
    Disdain, that torrent will devour
My vulture-hopes; and he's possess'd
Of heaven, that's but from hell released.

Then crown my joys or cure my pain:
Give me more love or more disdain.

Thomas Carew

177

TO A LADY ASKING HIM HOW LONG HE WOULD LOVE HER

It is not, darling, in our power
    To say how long our love will last;
It may be we, within this hour,
    May lose those joys we now do taste.
The blessèd that immortal be
From change in love only are free.

Then, since we mortal lovers are,
    Ask not how long our love will last;
But, while it does, let us take care
    Each minute be with pleasure passed.
Were it not madness to deny
To live because we're sure to die?

Sir George Etheredge

Christopher Marlowe's "The Passionate Shepherd to His Love" was not only one of the most popular poems of the period but one of the most imitated. Sir Walter Raleigh answered Marlowe's opening line ("Come live with me and be my love") in the realistic argument of "The Nymph's Reply to the Shepherd" which begins:

If all the world and love were young,
And truth in every shepherd's tongue,
These pretty pleasures might me move
To live with you and be your love.

John Donne could not resist the temptation to turn Marlowe's love lyric into playful metaphors about fishing. Entitled "The Bait," Donne's imitation contains such charming stanzas as:

Come live with me and be my love,
And we will some new pleasure prove
Of golden sands and crystal brooks,
With silken lines and silver hooks . . .

When thou wilt swim in that live bath,
Each fish, which every channel hath,
Will amorously to thee swim,
Gladder to catch thee, than thou him.

If thou, to be seen, beest loath,
By sun or moon, thou dark'nest both;
And if myself hath leave to see.
I need not their light, having thee.

However, it is Marlowe's poem which has outlived all its imitations.

THE PASSIONATE SHEPHERD TO HIS LOVE

Come live with me and be my love,
And we will all the pleasures prove
That hills and valleys, dales and fields,
Or woods or steepy mountain yields.

And we will sit upon the rocks,
And see the shepherds feed their flocks
By shallow rivers, to whose falls
Melodious birds sing madrigals.

And I will make thee beds of roses
And a thousand fragrant posies;
A cap of flowers, and a kirtle
Embroidered all with leaves of myrtle.

A gown made of the finest wool
Which from our pretty lambs we pull;
Fair-lined slippers for the cold,
With buckles of the purest gold.

A belt of straw and ivy-buds
With coral clasps and amber studs:
And if these pleasures may thee move,
Come live with me and be my love.

The shepherd swains shall dance and sing
For thy delight each May morning:
If these delights thy mind may move,
Then live with me and be my love.

Christopher Marlowe

Shakespeare's one hundred and fifty-four sonnets are the most intimate of all his works. There has been continual controversy concerning the story behind the poems—it has been questioned whether there is a story at all—but there is no doubt about the personal ecstasy and agony. In the plays—"all the world's a stage"—Shakespeare revealed a vast pageant of extraordinary characters; in the sonnets he revealed himself. "With this key," said Wordsworth, "Shakespeare unlocked his heart." "Here," wrote the critic George Brandes, "and here alone, we see Shakespeare himself, distinct from his other creations—loving, admiring, longing, tortured, humiliated, and adoring."

MARRIAGE OF TRUE MINDS

Let me not to the marriage of true minds
Admit impediments. Love is not love
Which alters when it alteration finds,
Or bends with the remover to remove.
O no! it is an ever-fixed mark
That looks on tempests, and is never shaken;
It is the star to every wandering bark,

Whose worth's unknown, although his height be taken.
Love's not Time's fool, though rosy lips and cheeks
Within his bending sickle's compass come;
Love alters not with his brief hours and weeks,
But bears it out even to the edge of doom.
  If this be error and upon me proved,
  I never writ, nor no man ever loved.

William Shakespeare

FORTUNE AND MEN'S EYES

When in disgrace with fortune and men's eyes
I all alone beweep my outcast state,
And trouble deaf heaven with my bootless cries,
And look upon myself and curse my fate,
Wishing me like to one more rich in hope,
Featured like him, like him with friends possessed,
Desiring this man's art, and that man's scope,
With what I most enjoy contented least;
Yet in these thoughts myself almost despising,
Haply I think on thee—and then my state,
Like to the lark at break of day arising
From sullen earth, sings hymns at heaven's gate;
  For thy sweet love remembered, such wealth brings
  That then I scorn to change my state with kings.

William Shakespeare

SHALL I COMPARE THEE?

Shall I compare thee to a summer's day?
Thou art more lovely and more temperate:
Rough winds do shake the darling buds of May,
And summer's lease hath all to short a date:
Sometime too hot the eye of heaven shines,
And often is his gold complexion dimm'd;
And every fair from fair sometime declines,
By chance or nature's changing course untrimm'd;
But thy eternal summer shall not fade,
Nor lose possession of that fair thou ow'st;

Nor shall Death brag thou wander'st in his shade,
When in eternal lines to time thou grow'st:
  So long as men can breathe, or eyes can see,
  So long lives this, and this gives life to thee.

William Shakespeare

DEVOURING TIME

Devouring Time, blunt thou the lion's paws,
And make the earth devour her own sweet brood;
Pluck the keen teeth from the fierce tiger's jaws,
And burn the long-lived phœnix in her blood;
Make glad and sorry seasons as thou fleet'st,
And do whate'er thou wilt, swift-footed Time,
To the wide world and all her fading sweets;
But I forbid thee one most heinous crime:
O, carve not with thy hours my love's fair brow,
Nor draw no lines there with thine antique pen;
Him in thy course untainted do allow
For beauty's pattern to succeeding men.
  Yet do thy worst, old Time: despite thy wrong,
  My love shall in my verse ever live young.

William Shakespeare

HOW LIKE A WINTER

How like a winter hath my absence been
From thee, the pleasure of the fleeting year!
What freezings have I felt! What dark days seen!
What old December's bareness everywhere!
And yet this time removed was summer's time;
The teeming autumn, big with rich increase,
Bearing the wanton burthen of the prime,
Like widowed wombs after their lords' decease:
Yet this abundant issue seemed to me
But hope of orphans and unfathered fruit;
For summer and his pleasures wait on thee,
And, thou away, the very birds are mute;
  Or, if they sing, 'tis with so dull a cheer
  That leaves look pale, dreading the winter's near.

William Shakespeare

WHEN MY LOVE SWEARS

When my love swears that she is made of truth,
I do believe her, though I know she lies,
That she might think me some untutored youth,
Unlearnéd in the world's false subtleties.
Thus vainly thinking that she thinks me young,
Although she knows my days are past the best,
Simply I credit her false-speaking tongue:
On both sides thus is simple truth suppressed.
But wherefore says she not she is unjust?
And wherefore say not I that I am old?
O, love's best habit is in seeming trust,
And age in love loves not to have years told.
    Therefore I lie with her and she with me,
    And in our faults by lies we flattered be.

William Shakespeare

FAREWELL!

Farewell! thou art too dear for my possessing,
And like enough thou know'st thy estimate:
The charter of thy worth gives thee releasing;
My bonds in thee are all determinate.
For how do I hold thee but by thy granting?
And for that riches where is my deserving?
The cause of this fair gift in me is wanting,
And so my patent back again is swerving.
Thyself thou gavest, thy own worth then not knowing,
Or me, to whom thou gavest it, else mistaking;
So thy great gift, upon misprision growing,
Comes home again, on better judgement making.
    Thus have I had thee, as a dream doth flatter,
    In sleep a king, but waking no such matter.

William Shakespeare

O MISTRESS MINE

O Mistress mine, where are you roaming?
O, stay and hear—your true love's coming,
    That can sing both high and low.
Trip no further, pretty sweeting;
Journeys end in lovers' meeting,
    Every wise man's son doth know.

What is love? 'tis not hereafter;
Present mirth hath present laughter;
  What's to come is still unsure:
In delay there lies no plenty—
Then come kiss me, sweet-and-twenty,
  Youth's a stuff will not endure.

William Shakespeare

WHY SHOULD WE DELAY?

Phyllis! why should we delay
Pleasures shorter than the day?
Could we (which we never can!)
Stretch our lives beyond their span,
Beauty like a shadow flies,
And our youth before us dies.
Or, would youth and beauty stay,
Love hath wings, and will away.
Love hath swifter wings than Time:
Change in love to Heaven does climb.
Gods, that never change their state,
Vary oft their love and hate.

Phyllis! to this truth we owe
All the love betwixt us two:
Let not you and I inquire
What has been our past desire;
On what shepherd you have smiled,
Or what nymphs I have beguiled.
Leave it to the planets, too,
What we shall hereafter do.
For the joys we now may prove,
Take advice of present love.

Edmund Waller

Little is known about Bartholomew Griffin. His birth date is a conjecture and his career is uncertain. He was the author of a sonnet sequence printed in an Elizabethan miscellany, one of the sonnets being credited to Shakespeare. "Her Heart" is a curiosity as well as a poignant love poem, a tour de force with one word repeated fourteen times instead of the customary variation of rhymes.

HER HEART

Fly to her heart, hover about her heart,
With dainty kisses mollify her heart;
Pierce with thy arrows her obdurate heart;
With sweet allurements ever move her heart;
At mid-day and at midnight touch her heart;
Be lurking closely, nestle about her heart;
With power (thou art a god) command her heart;
Kindle thy coals of love about her heart;
Yea, even into thyself transform her heart.
Ah, she must love! Be sure thou have her heart,
And I must die if thou have not her heart.
Thy bed, if thou rest well, must be her heart;
He hath the best part sure that hath the heart.
What have I not, if I have but her heart!

Bartholomew Griffin

Andrew Marvell's "To His Coy Mistress" is a miracle of paradox. It is both worldly and detached from the world; it is conversational and yet rhetorical; contemporary but, somehow, classical. It begins with casual light-heartedness, airy play, and gradually the play becomes serious, mounts from wit to passion, to compulsive love and need, and finally to a revenge upon Time, the Sun that refuses to stand still.

TO HIS COY MISTRESS

Had we but world enough, and time,
This coyness, lady, were no crime.
We would sit down, and think which way
To walk, and pass our long love's day.
Thou by the Indian Ganges' side
Should'st rubies find: I by the tide

Of Humber would complain. I would
Love you ten years before the Flood,
And you should, if you please, refuse
Till the conversion of the Jews.
My vegetable love should grow
Vaster than empires, and more slow.
An hundred years should go to praise
Thine eyes, and on thy forehead gaze:
Two hundred to adore each breast:
But thirty thousand to the rest;
An age at least to every part,
And the last age should show your heart.
For, lady, you deserve this state,
Nor would I love at lower rate.

   But at my back I always hear
Time's wingéd chariot hurrying near:
And yonder all before us lie
Deserts of vast eternity.
Thy beauty shall no more be found;
Nor, in thy marble vault, shall sound
My echoing song: then worms shall try
That long-preserved virginity,
And your quaint honor turn to dust,
And into ashes all my lust.
The grave's a fine and private place,
But none, I think, do there embrace.
   Now, therefore, while the youthful hue
Sits on thy skin like morning dew,
And while thy willing soul transpires
At every pore with instant fires,
Now let us sport us while we may;
And now, like amorous birds of prey,
Rather at once our Time devour,
Than languish in his slow-chapt power.[1]
Let us roll all our strength and all
Our sweetness up into one ball,
And tear our pleasures with rough strife
Thorough the iron gates of life.
Thus, though we cannot make our Sun
Stand still, yet we will make him run.

Andrew Marvell

[1] Slow-chapt power: slow-devouring paws.

LOVE WILL FIND OUT THE WAY

Over the mountains
  And over the waves,
Under the fountains
  And under the graves,
Under floods that are deepest,
  Which Neptune obey,
Over rocks that are steepest
  Love will find out the way.

You may esteem him
  A child for his might,
Or you may deem him
  A coward for his flight;
But if she, whom love doth honor,
  Be concealed from the day,
Set a thousand guards upon her,
  Love will find out the way.

Some think to lose him
  By having him confined;
And some do suppose him,
  Poor thing, to be blind.
But if ne'er so close you wall him,
  Do the best that you may,
Blind love, if so you call him,
  Will find out the way.

You may train the eagle
  To stoop to your fist;
Or you may inveigle
  The phoenix from her nest;
The lioness, you may move her
  To give over her prey;
But you'll ne'er stop a lover:
  He will find out the way.

Anonymous

WHISTLE AN' I'LL COME

O whistle an' I'll come to ye, my lad,
O whistle an' I'll come to ye, my lad;
Tho' father an' mither an a' should go mad,
O whistle an' I'll come to ye, my lad.

But warily tent[1] when ye come to court me,
And come nae unless the back-yett be a-jee[2];
Syne[3] up the back-stile, and let naebody see,
And come as ye were na comin to me,
And come as ye were na comin to me.
    O whistle an' I'll come, etc.

At kirk, or at market, whene'er ye meet me,
Gang by me as tho' that ye car'd na a flie;
But steal me a blink o' your bonie black e'e,
Yet look as ye were na lookin to me,
Yet look as ye were na lookin to me.
    O whistle an' I'll come, etc.

[1] Tent: take care.
[2] Back-yett be a-jee: back-gate be ajar.
[3] Syne: then.

Aye vow and protest that ye care na for me,
And whiles ye may lightly my beauty a-wee;
But court na anither, tho' jokin ye be,
For fear that she wile your fancy frae me,
For fear that she wile your fancy frae me.
    O whistle and I'll come, etc.

Robert Burns

LOVE'S PHILOSOPHY

The fountains mingle with the river,
    And the rivers with the Ocean,
The winds of Heaven mix for ever
    With a sweet emotion;
Nothing in the world is single:
    All things by a law divine
In one spirit meet and mingle.
    Why not I with thine?

See the mountains kiss high Heaven
    And the waves clasp one another;
No sister flower would be forgiven
    If it disdained its brother;
And the sunlight clasps the earth
    And the moonbeams kiss the sea;
What is all this sweet work worth
    If thou kiss not me?

Percy Bysshe Shelley

I KNOW WHO I LOVE

I know where I'm going;
And I know who's going with me;
I know who I love,
But the dear knows who I'll marry.

I have stockings of silk,
Shoes of fine green leather,
Combs to buckle my hair,
And a ring for every finger.

Feather beds are soft,
And painted rooms are bonny—
But I would leave them all
To go with my love Johnny.

Some say he's black,
But I say he's bonny,
The fairest of them all,
My handsome, winsome Johnny.

I know where I'm going;
And I know who's going with me;
I know who I love,
But the dear knows who I'll marry.

Anonymous

A WOMAN'S LAST WORD

Let's contend no more, love,
 Strive nor weep:
All be as before, love,
 —Only sleep!

What so wild as words are?
 I and thou
In debate, as birds are,
 Hawk on bough!

See the creature stalking
 While we speak!
Hush and hide the talking,
 Cheek on cheek!

What so false as truth is,
 False to thee?
Where the serpent's tooth is,
 Shun the tree—

Where the apple reddens
 Never pry—
Lest we lose our Edens,
 Eve and I!

Be a god and hold me
    With a charm!
Be a man and fold me
    With thine arm!

Teach me, only teach, love!
    As I ought
I will speak thy speech, love,
    Think thy thought—

Meet, if thou require it,
    Both demands,
Laying flesh and spirit
    In thy hands.

That shall be tomorrow,
    Not tonight;
I must bury sorrow
    Out of sight.

Must a little weep, love,
    (Foolish me)
And so fall asleep, love,
    Loved by thee.

Robert Browning

THE MOTH'S KISS, FIRST!

The moth's kiss, first!
Kiss me as if you made believe
You were not sure, this eve,
How my face, your flower, had pursed
Its petals up; so, here and there
You brush it, till I grow aware
Who wants me, and wide ope I burst.

The bee's kiss, now!
Kiss me as if you enter'd gay
My heart at some noonday,
A bud that dares not disallow
The claim, so all is render'd up,
And passively its shatter'd cup
Over your head to sleep I bow.

Robert Browning

IN LOVE, IF LOVE BE LOVE

In Love, if Love be Love, if Love be ours,
Faith and unfaith can ne'er be equal powers:
Unfaith in aught is want of faith in all.

It is the little rift within the lute,
That by and by will make the music mute,
And ever widening slowly silence all.

The little rift within the lover's lute
Or little pitted speck in garnered fruit,
That rotting inward slowly moulders all.

It is not worth the keeping: let it go:
But shall it? answer, darling, answer, no.
And trust me· not at all or all in all.

Alfred, Lord Tennyson

NOW SLEEPS THE CRIMSON PETAL

Now sleeps the crimson petal, now the white,
Nor waves the cypress in the palace walk:
Nor winks the gold fin in the porphyry font.
The firefly wakens. Waken thou with me.

Now droops the milk-white peacock like a ghost,
And like a ghost she glimmers on to me.

Now lies the Earth all Danaë to the stars,
And all thy heart lies open unto me.

Now slides the silent meteor on, and leaves
A shining furrow, as thy thoughts in me.

Now folds the lily all her sweetness up,
And slips into the bosom of the lake;
So fold thyself, my dearest, thou, and slip
Into my bosom and be lost in me.

Alfred, Lord Tennyson

NOW!

Out of your whole life give but a moment!
  All of your life that has gone before,
  All to come after it,—so you ignore,
So you make perfect the present; condense,
In a rapture of rage, for perfection's endowment,
Thought and feeling and soul and sense,
Merged in a moment which gives me at last
You around me for once, you beneath me, above me—
Me, sure that, despite of time future, time past,
This tick of life-time's one moment you love me!
How long such suspension may linger? Ah, Sweet,
  The moment eternal—just that and no more—
  When ecstasy's utmost we clutch at the core,
While cheeks burn, arms open, eyes shut, and lips meet!

Robert Browning

HEART'S DESIRE

A Book of Verses underneath the Bough,
A Jug of Wine, a Loaf of Bread—and Thou
Beside me singing in the Wilderness—
Oh, Wilderness were Paradise enow!

Ah Love, could you and I with Him conspire
To grasp this sorry Scheme of Things entire,
Would not we shatter it to bits—and then
Remould it nearer to the Heart's desire!

Omar Khayyám-Fitzgerald

193

*It has been said that Baudelaire made a science of mixing sensuality
and perversity. His most characteristic lines are surcharged with pas-
sionate fantasies in which beauty often turns into brutality; he found
no subject too sordid or too sacrosanct. A long contemplation with evil
made him call his most important work Fleurs du Mal. Yet nothing
Baudelaire wrote was without vision, a mystical fire which, as Swin-
burne wrote, "feeds our hearts with flame."*

PARFUM EXOTIQUE

When, with eyes closed in an autumnal dream,
I breathe the fragrance of your sultry breast,
I see in vision hell's infernal stream
And sunset fires that have no instant's rest:
An idle island where the unnatural scheme
Of Nature is by savorous fruits oppressed,
And where man's body is the woman's guest,
And women's bodies are not what they seem.

Drawn by your odor like exotic gales,
I see a harbor filled with masts and sails,
Wearied by waves and winds that weary me—
And in the perfume of the tamarind there clings
I know not what of marvelous luxury,
Mixed in my soul with chants a sailor sings.

Charles Baudelaire
translated by Arthur Symons

YOUR KISSES

Your kisses, and the way you curl,
Delicious and distracting girl,
Into one's arms and round about,
Inextricably in and out,
Twining luxuriously, as twine
The clasping tangles of the vine;
So loving to be loved, so gay
And greedy for our holiday:
A little tossing sea of sighs,
Till the slow calm seal up your eyes.

And then how prettily you sleep.
You nestle close and let me keep
My folded fingers in the nest
Of your warm comfortable breast.
And as I dream, lying awake,
Of sleep well wasted for your sake,
I feel the very pulse and heat
Of your young life-blood beat, and beat
With mine. And you are mine, my sweet!

Arthur Symons

LOVE AND SLEEP

Lying asleep between the strokes of night,
I saw my love lean over my sad bed,
Pale as the duskiest lily's leaf or head,
Smooth-skinned and dark, with bare throat to invite,
Too wan for blushing and too warm for white,
But perfect-colored without white or red.
And her lips opened amorously, and said—
I knew not what—saving one word: Delight.

And all her face was honey to my mouth,
And all her body pasture to my eyes:
The long, lithe arms and hands hotter than fire,
The quivering flanks, hair smelling of the south,
The bright light feet, the splendid supple thighs,
And glittering eyelids of my soul's desire.

Algernon Charles Swinburne

SONG

Love laid his sleepless head
On a thorny rosy bed;
And his eyes with tears were red,
And pale his lips as the dead.

And fear and sorrow and scorn
Kept watch by his head forlorn,
Till the night was overworn,
And the world was merry with morn.

And Joy came up with the day,
And kissed Love's lips as he lay,
And the watchers ghostly and gray
Sped from his pillow away.

And his eyes as the dawn grew bright,
And his lips waxed ruddy as light:
Sorrow may reign for a night,
But day shall bring back delight.

Algernon Charles Swinburne

Although the plays of J. M. Synge were written in prose, they were couched in an enriched vocabulary and a splendor of imagery that could have been accomplished only by a poet. His Poems and Translations, published after his death, vibrate with the same racy vigor that quickened The Playboy of the Western World.

IN MAY

In a nook
That opened south,
You and I
Lay mouth to mouth.

A snowy gull
And sooty daw
Came and looked
With many a caw;

"Such," I said,
"Are I and you,
When you've kissed me
Black and blue!"

J. M. Synge

THE TIRED WOMAN

O my lover, blind me;
Take your cords and bind me.
Then drive me through a silent land
With the compelling of your open hand.

There is too much of sound, too much for sight,
In thunderous lightnings of this night;
There is too much of freedom for my feet,
Bruised by the stones of this disordered street.

I know that there is sweetest rest for me
In silent fields and in captivity.
O lover, drive me through a stilly land
With the compelling of your open hand.

Anna Wickham

Theodore Roethke's reckless exuberance frequently brought him to the pitch of madness. In his manic state he achieved some of his finest effects. Poetry was Roethke's therapy; it helped if it did not wholly heal the sick man with the power of pure, sensuous form.

I KNEW A WOMAN

I knew a woman, lovely in her bones,
When small birds sighed, she would sigh back at them;
Ah, when she moved, she moved more ways than one:
The shapes a bright container can contain!
Of her choice virtues only gods should speak,
Or English poets who grew up on Greek
(I'd have them sing in chorus, cheek to cheek).

How well her wishes went! She stroked my chin,
She taught me Turn, and Counter-turn, and Stand;
She taught me Touch, that undulant white skin;
I nibbled meekly from her proffered hand;
She was the sickle; I, poor I, the rake,
Coming behind her for her pretty sake
(But what prodigious mowing we did make).

Love likes a gander, and adores a goose:
Her full lips pursed, the errant note to seize;
She played it quick, she played it light and loose;
My eyes, they dazzled at her flowing knees;
Her several parts could keep a pure repose,
Or one hip quiver with a mobile nose
(She moved in circles, and those circles moved).

Let seed be grass, and grass turn into hay:
I'm martyr to a motion not my own;
What's freedom for? To know eternity.
I swear she cast a shadow white as stone.
But who would count eternity in days?
These old bones live to learn her wanton ways:
(I measure time by how a body sways).

Theodore Roethke

A songwriter, a singer, and a novelist, Leonard Cohen is, first of all, a poet. Born in Canada, he became popular because of his music, his imagery, and his confessional intimacy. Like his public performances, his private poems are touched with personal warmth.

TRAVEL

Loving you, flesh to flesh, I often thought
Of travelling penniless to some mud throne
Where a master might instruct me how to plot
My life away from pain, to love alone
In the bruiseless embrace of stone and lake.

Lost in the fields of your hair I was never lost
Enough to lose a way I had to take;
Breathless beside your body I could not exhaust
The will that forbid me contract, vow,
Or promise, and often while you slept
I looked in awe beyond your beauty.

                                        Now
I know why many men have stopped and wept
Half-way between the loves they leave and seek,
And wondered if travel leads them anywhere—
Horizons keep the soft line of your cheek,
The windy sky's a locket for your hair.

                              Leonard Cohen

Anne Sexton plunges into poetry with unrestrained excitement. In the following poem, the climax of a sequence entitled "Eighteen Days Without You," she exults in the boomerang-like return of her lover.

DECEMBER 18th

Swift boomerang, come get!
I am delicate. You've been gone.
The losing has hurt me some, yet
I must bend for you. See me arch. I'm turned on.
My eyes are lawn-colored, my hair brunette.

Kiss the package, Mr. Bind!
Yes, Would you consider hurling yourself
upon me, rigorous but somehow kind?
I am laid out like paper on your cabin kitchen shelf.
So draw me a breast. I like to be underlined.

Look, lout! Say yes!
Draw me like a child. I shall need
merely two round eyes and a small kiss.
A small o. Two earrings would be nice. Then proceed
to the shoulder. You may pause at this.

Catch me. I'm your disease.
Please go slow all along the torso
drawing beads and mouths and trees
and o's, a little *graffiti* and a small *hello*
for I grab, I nibble, I lift, I please.

Draw me good, draw me warm.
Bring me your raw-boned wrist and your
strange, Mr. Bind, strange stubborn horn.
Darling, bring with this an hour of undulations, for
this is the music for which I was born.

Lock in! Be alert, my acrobat
and I will be soft wood and you the nail
and we will make fiery ovens for Jack Sprat
and you will hurl yourself into my tiny jail
and we will take a supper together and that
will be that.

Anne Sexton

The
Mystery
of
Love

Love begins and ends in mystery, "a wonder and a wild desire." The griefs and raptures, the tribulations and triumphs, are equally mysterious. Mystery inspires Keats' heavy-hearted fourteen lines and Elizabeth Barrett Browning's overbrimming sonnets with magic power. It illuminates the sense of transmigration in Dante Gabriel Rossetti's "Sudden Light" and Poe's trance-like lyric "To One in Paradise":

> In what ethereal dances
>   By what eternal streams.

It is not bound by time. It reverberates through Shelley's "Music, when soft voices die" and, a hundred years later, through Conrad Aiken's:

> Music I heard with you was more than music,
> And bread I broke with you was more than bread.

Coleridge summed it all up in four lines that evoke the mastery as well as the mystery of man's most profound emotion:

> All thoughts, all passions, all delights,
> Whatever stirs this mortal frame,
> All are but ministers of love,
> And feed his sacred flame.

I HEAR SOME SAY

> I hear some say, "This man is not in love!"
> "Who? Can he love? A likely thing!" they say.
> "Read but his verse, and it will easily prove!"
> O judge not rashly, gentle sir, I pray!
> Because I loosely trifle in this sort,
> As one that fain his sorrows would beguile,
> You now suppose me, all this time, in sport,
> And please yourself with this conceit the while.

Ye shallow censors! Sometimes, see ye not,
In greatest perils some men pleasant be?
Where Fame by death is only to be got,
They resolute! So stands the case with me.
  Where other men in depth of passion cry,
  I laugh at Fortune, as in jest to die!

Michael Drayton

WHEN MEN SHALL FIND THY FLOWER

When men shall find thy flower, thy glory, pass,
And thou, with careful brow sitting alone,
Receivéd hast this message from thy glass,
That tells the truth and says that all is gone;
Fresh shalt thou see in me the wounds thou madest,
Though spent thy flame, in me the heat remaining;
I that have loved thee thus before thou fadest,
My faith shall wax when thou art in thy waning.

The world shall find this miracle in me,
That fire can burn when all the matter's spent;
Then what my faith hath been, thyself shall see,
And that thou wast unkind, thou mayst repent.
Thou mayst repent that thou hast scorned my tears,
When winter snows upon thy sable hairs.

Samuel Daniel

MUSIC, WHEN SOFT VOICES DIE

Music, when soft voices die,
Vibrates in the memory;
Odors, when sweet violets sicken,
Live within the sense they quicken.

Rose leaves, when the rose is dead,
Are heap'd for the belovéd's bed;
And so thy thoughts, when thou art gone,
Love itself shall slumber on.

Percy Bysshe Shelley

BRIGHT STAR

Bright star, would I were stedfast as thou art—
  Not in lone splendour hung aloft the night
And watching, with eternal lids apart,
  Like nature's patient, sleepless Eremite,
The moving waters at their priestlike task
  Of pure ablution round earth's human shores,
Or gazing on the new soft-fallen mask
  Of snow upon the mountains and the moors—
No—yet still stedfast, still unchangeable,
  Pillow'd upon my fair love's ripening breast,
To feel for ever its soft fall and swell,
  Awake for ever in a sweet unrest,
Still, still to hear her tender-taken breath,
And so live ever—or else swoon to death.

John Keats

Rainer Maria Rilke, ranked by many as the greatest of modern German poets, was, by a geographical irony, born in Czechoslovakia and died in Switzerland. A poet of the most exquisite sensibility, his was a clairvoyant vision expressed in a half-mystical, half-casual idiom.

LOVE-SONG

How can I hinder or restrain my soul
So that it does not yearn for yours? And how
Can it be lured to life apart from you?
Gladly would I (had I complete control)
Transport it, a dark secret thing, to new
And untried depths of silence. But I know
How everything that stirs me, stirs you too;
How you and I are like a bow that's bound,
Though with two strings, to give a single sound.
Upon what instrument have we been spanned?
And what strange player plays us, heart and hand?
O long, sweet song!

Rainer Maria Rilke
translated by Louis Untermeyer

Elizabeth Barrett Browning's Sonnets from the Portuguese are not, as the title might suggest, translations. Some of the most impassioned love poems ever written by a wife to her husband were so called because Robert Browning liked to tease his wife about her olive complexion by calling her "my little Portuguese." The sonnets themselves breathe a devotion that is close to idolatry.

HOW DO I LOVE THEE?

How do I love thee? Let me count the ways.
I love thee to the depth and breadth and height
My soul can reach, when feeling out of sight
For the ends of Being and ideal Grace.
I love thee to the level of every day's
Most quiet need, by sun and candlelight.
I love thee freely, as men strive for Right;
I love thee purely, as they turn from Praise.
I love thee with the passion put to use
In my old griefs, and with my childhood's faith.
I love thee with a love I seemed to lose
With my lost saints,—I love thee with the breath,
Smiles, tears, of all my life!—and, if God choose,
I shall but love thee better after death.

Elizabeth Barrett Browning

IF THOU MUST LOVE ME

If thou must love me, let it be for naught
Except for love's sake only. Do not say,
"I love her for her smile—her look—her way
Of speaking gently—for a trick of thought
That falls in well with mine, and certes brought
A sense of pleasant ease on such a day"—
For these things in themselves, Belovéd, may
Be changed, or change for thee—and love, so wrought,
May be unwrought so. Neither love me for
Thine own dear pity's wiping my cheeks dry—
A creature might forget to weep, who bore
Thy comfort long, and lose thy love thereby!
But love me for love's sake, that evermore
Thou may'st love on, through love's eternity.

Elizabeth Barrett Browning

WHEN OUR TWO SOULS STAND UP

When our two souls stand up erect and strong,
Face to face, silent, drawing nigh and nigher,
Until the lengthening wings break into fire
At either curvéd point,—what bitter wrong
Can the earth do to us, that we should not long
Be here contented? Think. In mounting higher,
The angels would press on us and aspire
To drop some golden orb of perfect song
Into our deep, dear silence. Let us stay
Rather on earth, Belovéd,—where the unfit,
Contrarious moods of men recoil away
And isolate pure spirits, and permit
A place to stand and love in for a day,
With darkness and the death-hour rounding it.

Elizabeth Barrett Browning

206

SUDDEN LIGHT

I have been here before,
    But when or how I cannot tell:
I know the grass beyond the door,
    The sweet keen smell,
The sighing sound, the lights around the shore.

You have been mine before—
    How long ago I may not know;
But just when at that swallow's soar
    Your neck turned so,
Some veil did fall—I knew it all of yore.

Has this been thus before?
    And shall not thus time's eddying flight
Still with our lives our love restore
    In death's despite?
And day and night yield one delight once more?

Dante Gabriel Rossetti

TO ONE IN PARADISE

Thou wast that all to me, love,
    For which my soul did pine—
A green isle in the sea, love,
    A fountain and a shrine,
All wreathed with fairy fruits and flowers,
    And all the flowers were mine.

Ah, dream too bright to last!
    Ah, starry Hope! that didst arise
But to be overcast!
    A voice from out the Future cries,
"On! on!"—but o'er the Past
    (Dim gulf!) my spirit hovering lies
Mute, motionless, aghast!

207

For, alas! alas! with me
    The light of Life is o'er!
No more—no more—no more—
    (Such language holds the solemn sea
To the sands upon the shore)
    Shall bloom the thunder-blasted tree,
Or the stricken eagle soar!

And all my days are trances,
    And all my nightly dreams
Are where thy grey eye glances,
    And where thy footstep gleams—
In what ethereal dances,
    By what eternal streams.

Edgar Allan Poe

With typical New England reticence Robert Frost expressed his background and himself in understatements and quiet but penetrating metaphors. He wrote few love poems. This is one of them, perhaps the subtlest and the most alluring.

THE SILKEN TENT

She is as in a field a silken tent
At midday when a sunny summer breeze
Has dried the dew and all its ropes relent,
So that in guys it gently sways at ease,
And its supporting central cedar pole,
That is its pinnacle to heavenward
And signifies the sureness of the soul,
Seems to owe naught to any single cord,
But strictly held by none, is loosely bound
By countless silken ties of love and thought
To everything on earth the compass round,
And only by one's going slightly taut
In the capriciousness of summer air
Is of the slightest bondage made aware.

Robert Frost

The name of Francis William Bourdillon, a late nineteenth-century versifier, survives because of a single lyric. The following eight lines are all of his works that appear in anthologies and dictionaries of quotations.

THE NIGHT HAS A THOUSAND EYES

The night has a thousand eyes,
　And the day but one;
Yet the light of the bright world dies
　With the dying sun.

The mind has a thousand eyes,
　And the heart but one;
Yet the light of a whole life dies
　When love is done.

Francis William Bourdillon

Almost half a century before he built the enormously complicated Cantos, Ezra Pound was writing lyrics in the manner of medieval singers. He was in his mid-twenties when he composed the nostalgic music of "A Virginal."

A VIRGINAL

No, No! Go from me. I have left her lately.
I will not spoil my sheath with lesser brightness,
For my surrounding air has a new lightness;
Slight are her arms, yet they have bound me straitly
And left me cloaked as with a gauze of ether;
As with sweet leaves; as with a subtle clearness.
Oh, I have picked up magic in her nearness
To sheathe me half in half the things that sheathe her.

No, no! Go from me. I have still the flavor,
Soft as spring wind that's come from birchen bowers.
Green come the shoots, aye April in the branches,
As winter's wound with her sleight hand she staunches,
Hath of the trees a likeness of the savor:
As white their bark, so white this lady's hours.

Ezra Pound

Author of twenty-two volumes of poetry and six of prose, Kenneth Patchen was ignored by the literary establishment until The Collected Poems was published in his mid-fifties. He then received a ten-thousand-dollar award for his "lifelong contribution to American letters" and was hailed as one who not only wrote some of the most touching poems of his time but also acted as "one of the most articulate spokesmen for the human imagination in an age when reason seems to have gone awry."

FOR MIRIAM

Do I not deal with angels
When her lips I touch

So gentle, so warm and sweet—falsity
Has no sight of her.

O the world is a place of veils and roses
When she is there.

I am come to her wonder
Like a boy finding a star in a haymow
And there is nothing cruel or mad or evil
Anywhere.

Kenneth Patchen

210

Conrad Aiken's Collected Poems runs to eight hundred and ninety-five pages. Yet some of his richest writings are in books that appeared after what many critics has assumed was Aiken's ultimate work. "The Lovers" is one of fifty poems included in The Morning Song of Lord Zero, published in his seventy fourth year.

THE LOVERS

This painful love dissect to the last shred:
abjure it, it will not be solved in bed;
agony of the senses, but compounded
of soul's dream, heart's wish, blood's will, all confounded
with hate, despair, distrust, the fear of each
for what the other brings of alien speech.
Self-love, my love, no farther goes than this,
that when we kiss, it is ourselves we kiss.

O eyes no eyes, but fountains fraught with tears,
o heart no heart, but cistern of the years,
how backward now to childhood's spring we thrust
there to uncover the green shoots of lust:
how forward then to the bare skull we look
to taste our passion dead in doomsday book!
Self-love is all we know, my love, and this
breeds all these worlds, and kills them, when we kiss.

Yet would I give, yet would you take, a time
where self-love were no criminal, no crime:
where the true godhead in each self discovers
that the self-lovers are both gods and lovers.
O love, of this wise love no word be said,
it will be solved in a diviner bed,
where the divine dance teaches self-love this,
that when we kiss it is a god we kiss.

Conrad Aiken

INDEXES

Poem Titles

A Birthday, 137
A Bowl of Roses, 9
A Dream within a Dream, 83
A Farewell, 92
A Reasonable Affliction, 51
A Red, Red Rose, 165
A Subaltern's Love-Song, 62
A True Maid, 49
A Virginal, 209
A Woman's Last Word, 190
A World Still Young, 8
Adam, Lilith, and Eve, 53
Advice to a Girl, 35
Ae Fond Kiss, 80
All or Nothing, 47
All Seasons in One, 31
All the Tree's Hands, 146
An Arab Love-Song, 168
"And Forgive Us Our Trespasses",
  45
Answer to Jealousy, 48
Ask Me No More (Carew), 163
Ask Me No More (Tennyson), 85
Awake! Awake!, 3
Away with Silks, 22

Ballade, 144
Ballade for a Bridegroom, 131
Ballade of the Women of Paris, 130
Barbara Allen, 112

Beauty Is Not Bound, 14
Beauty's Self, 13
Behold, Thou Art Fair, 157
Belinda the Charitable, 37
Break of Day, 76
Bredon Hill, 99
Bright Star, 204
By What Sweet Name, 52

Capsule Conclusions, 64
Cards for Kisses, 37
Catch a Falling Star, 38
Come, My Celia, 16
Come Slowly, Eden!, 86
Crystal Anniversary, 148

Day Dream, 149
December 18th, 199
Delight in Disorder, 21
Devouring Time, 182
Dover Beach, 120
Drink to Me Only with Thine Eyes,
  152

Echo, 91
Elegy for a Mis-spent Youth, 106
Equals, 58

Faithful in My Fashion, 97
False and Fickle, 46
False though She Be, 47

Farewell (Byron), 83
Farewell! (Shakespeare), 183
Fear Not, Dear Love, 152
Finis?, 106
Folk-Song, 102
Follow Your Saint, 177
For Miriam, 210
Fortune and Men's Eyes, 181
Fulfillment, 135

Gather Ye Rosebuds, 19
Go, Lovely Rose!, 162
Good Advice, 36
Greensleeves, 74

Heart's Desire, 193
Her Heart, 185
How Do I Love Thee?, 205
How Like a Winter, 182
How Many Times?, 167
How She Resolved to Act, 59
How Sweet I Roamed, 77

I Cannot Live with You, 87
I Cry Your Mercy, 81
I Have Been through the Gates, 101
I Have No Life but This, 86
I Hear Some Say, 202
I Knew a Woman, 197
I Know Who I Love, 189
I Shall Have Had My Day, 137
If Thou Must Love Me, 205
Imperial Adam, 126
In Love, if Love Be Love, 192
In Love with Two, 69
In May, 196
In the Merry Month of May, 5
In the Spring-Time, 4
Is My Team Ploughing?, 119
It Was Out By Donnycarney, 10

Jenny Kissed Me, 23
June, 95

Kind Are Her Answers, 75
Kissin', 34

Less Than the Dust, 96
Let Us Live and Love, 175
Long Have I Borne Much, 68
Lord Randal, 108
Love and Sleep, 195
Love at First Sight, 3
Love on the Farm, 122
Love-Song, 204
Love Song from New England, 101
Love 20¢ the First Quarter Mile, 104
Love: Two Vignettes, 169
Love Will Find Out the Way, 187
Love's Constancy, 129
Love's Limit, 31
Love's Philosophy, 189
Love's Secret, 23

Man Is for the Woman Made, 45
Marriage of True Minds, 180
Meditation at Kew, 58
Meeting at Night, 115
Mementos, 105
Mine, 89
More Love or More Disdain, 177
More than Most Fair, 151
Mother, I Cannot Mind My Wheel, 84
Mourning Dove, 60
Muckle-Mouth Meg, 118
Music, When Soft Voices Die, 203
My Heart at Rest, 135
My Life Closed Twice, 89
My Life's Delight, 175
My Light Thou Art, 134
My True-Love Hath My Heart, 132

Neutral Tones, 94
Night Song at Amalfi, 57
"Not Marble, nor the Gilded Monuments", 143
Now!, 193
Now Sleeps the Crimson Petal, 192

O Mistress Mine, 183
O, No, John, 33
O Stay, Sweet Love, 32
O Sweetheart, Hear You, 10
O Wert Thou in the Cauld Blast, 154
O Western Wind, 160
Of All the Souls That Stand Create, 88
Oh, See How Thick the Goldcup Flowers, 56
Oh, When I Was in Love with You, 55
On a Girdle, 164

Parfum Exotique, 194
Porphyria's Lover, 116
Press Close Bare-Bosom'd Night, 169

Remember Me, 90
Renouncement, 139
Restrained Passion, 46
Romance, 139
Rondeau, 27
Rondel of Merciless Beauty, 70
Roundel of Farewell, 71

Sea Love, 100
Seals of Love, 74
Send Back My Heart, 132
Shall I Compare Thee?, 181
She Never Told Her Love, 73
She Walks in Beauty, 166
Sigh No More, 36
Silent Noon, 138
Since I Saw My Love, 142
Since There's No Help, 73
Sing, Ballad-Singer, 94
So Fast Entangled, 160
So White, So Soft, So Sweet, 16
Somewhere I Have Never Travelled, 26
Song, 195

Stop All the Clocks, 103
Such Sweet Neglect, 15
Sudden Light, 207
Suspicious Sweetheart, 54
Sweet Afton, 154
Sweet, Let Me Go, 44
Sweetest Love, I Do Not Go, 76

That Fond Impossibility, 42
That Reminds Me, 61
The Angry Lover, 49
The Banks O' Doon, 79
The Bracelet: To Julia, 19
The Bride, 18
The Cherry-Blossom Wand, 25
The Constant Lover, 43
The Dark Chamber, 140
The Dissembler, 50
The Douglas Tragedy, 109
The Effect of Love, 14
The Fired Pot, 125
The First Day, 8
The Forsaken Lover, 71
The Garden of Love, 78
"The Greek Anthology," 173
The Hill, 171
The Hope I Dreamed Of, 90
The Indian Serenade, 166
The Kiss, 54
The Lost Mistress, 113
The Lover Rejoiceth, 34
The Lovers, 211
The Man with a Hammer, 142
The Married Lover, 93
The Moth's Kiss, First!, 191
The Night Has a Thousand Eyes, 209
The Nightingale, 9
The Night-Piece: To Julia, 21
The Passionate Shepherd to His Love, 179
The Reconciliation, 30
The Silken Tent, 208
The Soul Selects Her Own Society, 86
The Sun Rising, 161

The Theft, 40
The Time I've Lost in Wooing, 51
The Time of Roses, 7
The Tired Man, 57
The Tired Woman, 197
The Touchstone, 41
The True Lover, 121
The Wife, 147
There Is a Lady, 160
This Tress, 24
To a Lady Asking Him How Long
    He Would Love Her, 178
To a Weeping Willow, 141
To Althea from Prison, 133
To Amarantha, 17
To Anthea, Who May Command
    Him Anything, 20
To Dream of Thee, 165
To Give My Love Good-Morrow, 6
To Helen, 168
To His Coy Mistress, 185
To Lucasta, on Going to the Wars,
    153
To One in Paradise, 207
Travel, 199
True Love, 63
Two in the Campagna, 114

Under the Willow-Shades, 42
Upon Julia's Clothes, 21

We'll Go No More A-Roving, 81
What Care I, 40
What Lips My Lips Have Kissed,
    102
When I Am Dead, 91
When I Was One-and-Twenty, 55
When Men Shall Find Thy Flower,
    203
When My Love Swears, 183
When Our Two Souls Stand Up,
    206
When We Court and Kiss, 176
When We Two Parted, 82
When You Are Old, 98
Whenever We Happen to Kiss, 54

Whistle an' I'll Come, 188
White in the Moon, 98
Why Should We Delay?, 184
Why So Pale and Wan?, 44
Wild Nights, 89
Winter Tryst, 145
With How Sad Steps, O Moon, 72

You, 130
You'll Love Me Yet, 7
Your Kisses (Symons), 24
Your Kisses (Symons), 194

Poets' Names

Aiken, Conrad, 202, 211
Appleman, Philip, 148
Arnold, Matthew, 108, 120, 121, 129
Auden, W. H., 61, 103

Baudelaire, Charles, 194
Beddoes, Thomas Lovell, 167
Behn, Aphra, 44, 45
Betjeman, John, 61, 62, 63
Bishop, Samuel, 41, 42
Blake, William, 23, 77
Bourdillon, Francis William, 208,
    209
Breton, Nicholas, 5
Brooke, Rupert, 67, 157, 171
Browning, Elizabeth Barrett, 24,
    202, 204, 205, 206
Browning, Robert, 7, 24, 53, 108,
    113, 114, 115, 116, 117, 118, 119,
    173, 190, 191, 193, 205
Burns, Robert, 79, 80, 151, 154, 155,
    157, 165, 188, 189
Byron, George Gordon, Lord, 22, 67,
    81, 82, 83, 157, 166, 167

Calkins, Clinch, 60
Campion, Thomas, 14, 35, 75, 76,
    173, 174, 175, 176, 177

Cardozo, Nancy, 149
Carew, Thomas, 36, 151, 152, 164, 173, 177
Cavendish, William, 129, 135, 136
Chaucer, Geoffrey, 70, 71, 130
Cohen, Leonard, 199
Coleridge, Samuel Taylor, 52, 202
Congreve, William, 29, 47, 48
Corkine, William, 44
Cory, Adela Florence. *See* Hope, Laurence.
Cummings, E. E., 26

Daniel, Samuel, 203
Davenant, William, 3, 42
De Kay, Ormonde, Jr., 145
Dickinson, Emily, 67, 85, 86, 87, 88, 89, 90
Donne, John, 29, 38, 39, 67, 76, 77, 157, 162, 178, 179
Dowson, Ernest, 97
Drayton, Michael, 67, 72, 73, 202, 203
Dryden, John, 46
D'Urfey, Thomas, 33

Etherege, Sir George, 178

Fearing, Kenneth, 104
FitzGerald, Edward, 193
Frost, Robert, 2, 208

Gay, John, 29
Griffin, Bartholomew, 185

Hardy, Thomas, 93, 94, 95
Heine, Heinrich, 54
Henley, W. E., 8
Herrick, Robert, 2, 12, 18, 19, 20, 21, 22
Heywood, Thomas, 5, 6
Hood, Thomas, 2, 7

Hope, A. D., 125, 126, 127
Hope, Laurence, 95, 96
Horace, 30, 31
Houseman, A. E., 55, 56, 98, 99, 100, 108, 119, 120, 121, 122
Hunt, Leigh, 22, 23

Jonson, Ben, 2, 12, 15, 16, 151, 152, 174
Joyce, James, 10

Keats, John, 16, 22, 67, 80, 81, 165, 202, 204
Khayyám, Omar. *See* Omar Khayyám.

Lamb, Charles, 5
Landor, Walter Savage, 84
Lawrence, D. H., 25, 122, 123, 124, 125
Levertov, Denise, 147
Levy, Amy, 95
Lewis, Michael, 106
Lovelace, Richard, 12, 16, 17, 42, 43, 129, 133, 134, 151, 153
Lyly, John, 29, 37

MacLeish, Archibald, 142, 143, 144
Marlowe, Christopher, 2, 3, 67, 69, 70, 178, 179, 180
Marvell, Andrew, 173, 185, 186
Merrell, Marion. *See* Calkins, Clinch.
Mew, Charlotte, 100, 101
Meynell, Alice, 139
Millay, Edna St. Vincent, 101, 102
Milton, John, 12
Montagu, Lady Mary Wortley, 46, 47
Moore, Merrill, 59
Moore, Thomas, 12, 51, 52
Motteaux, Peter Anthony, 45

Nash, Ogden, 60, 61
Nichols, Jeannette, 146

Omar Khayyám, 193
Ovid, 67, 68, 69, 70

Patchen, Kenneth, 210
Patmore, Coventry, 54, 92, 93
Payne, John, 71
Poe, Edgar Allen, 83, 84, 168, 202, 207, 208
Pope, Alexander, 29, 46, 125
Pound, Ezra, 209
Prior, Matthew, 29, 48, 49, 50, 51

Raleigh, Sir Walter, 178
Reeves, James, 33
Rilke, Ranier Maria, 204
Robinson, Clement, 74, 75
Roethke, Theodore, 197, 198
Rossetti, Christina Georgina, 2, 8, 67, 90, 91, 92, 129, 137, 138
Rossetti, Dante Gabriel, 8, 138, 139, 202, 207
Rossetti, William Michael, 8

Scott, Sir Walter, 29, 117
Sedley, Sir Charles, 134, 135
Sexton, Anne, 199, 200
Shakespeare, William, 3, 4, 5, 15, 36, 37, 47, 56, 73, 74, 142, 167, 173, 180, 181, 182, 183, 185
Shapiro, Karl, 144, 145
Shaw, George Bernard, 12
Shelley, Percy Bysshe, 16, 157, 166, 173, 189, 202, 203
Sidney, Sir Philip, 67, 72, 132
Snodgrass, W. D., 105
Spenser, Edmund, 151
Stallworthy, Jon, 106
Stevenson, Robert Louis, 139, 140
Suckling, Sir John, 16, 17, 18, 29, 43, 44, 132, 133

Swinburne, Algernon Charles, 2, 130, 131, 132, 173, 194, 195, 196
Symons, Arthur, 24, 173, 194, 195
Synge, J. M., 196

Teasdale, Sara, 57
Tennyson, Alfred, Lord, 84, 85, 137, 173, 192
Thompson, Francis, 157, 167, 168

Untermeyer, Louis, 27, 31, 54, 57, 58, 64, 65, 70, 102, 103, 140, 141, 174, 175, 204

Villon, François, 71, 130, 131, 132
Viorst, Judith, 63

Waller, Edmund, 162, 163, 164, 173, 184
Warren, Robert Penn, 169, 170
Welles, Winifred, 101
Whitman, Walt, 169, 173
Wickham, Anna, 12, 25, 26, 57, 58, 108, 125, 142, 197
Wilmot, John, Earl of Rochester, 129, 134
Wither, George, 29, 40, 41
Wordsworth, William, 180
Wyatt, Sir Thomas, 34, 35, 67, 71, 72

Yeats, William Butler, 10, 25, 98

First Lines

A Book of Verses underneath the Bough, 193
A fool and a knave with different views, 41
A frog under you, 147

A sweet disorder in the dress, 21
Ae fond kiss, and then we sever, 80
Alas! for all the pretty women who marry dull men, 58
Alas, my love, you do me wrong, 74
Albeit the Venice girls get praise, 130
All in the merry month of May, 112
All right. I may have lied to you and about you . . ., 104
All the tree's hands, 146
All's over, then: does truth sound bitter, 113
Amarantha, sweet and fair, 17
April is in my mistress' face, 31
As Chloe came into the room t'other day, 49
Ask me no more. The moon may draw the sea, 85
Ask me no more where Jove bestows, 163
At day break, when the falcon claps his wings, 131
Away with silks, away with lawn, 22

Back she came through the trembling dusk, 102
Behold, thou art fair, my love, 157
Belinda has such wond'rous charms, 37
Bid me to live, and I will live, 20
Breathless, we flung us on the windy hill, 171
Bright star, would I were steadfast as thou art—, 204
Busy old fool, unruly Sun, 161

Come live with me and be my love, 179
Come, my Celia, let us prove, 16
Come, O come, my life's delight, 175
Come slowly, Eden, 86
Come to me in the silence of the night, 91
Cupid and my Campaspe played, 37

Dawn, enemy of love, how slow you creep, 173
Dear Chloe, how blubbered is that pretty face, 48
Dear Colin, prevent my warm blushes, 46
Deep in a glassy ball, the future looks, 148
Devouring Time, blunt thou the lion's paws, 182
Do I not deal with angels, 210
Do you recall what I recall, 27
Drink to me only with thine eyes, 152

Fair Iris I love, and hourly I die, 46
Fair Selinda goes to prayers, 47
False though she be to me and love, 47
Farewell, I say, with tearful eye, 71
Farewell! if ever fondest prayer, 83
Farewell! thou art too dear for my possessing, 183
Fear not, dear love, that I'll reveal, 152
Flow gently, sweet Afton! among thy green braes, 154
Fly to her heart, hover about her heart, 185
Follow your saint, follow with accents sweet, 177
Frowned the Laird, on the Lord: "So, redhanded I catch thee, 118

Gather ye rosebuds while ye may, 19
Give beauty all her right, 14
Give me more love or more disdain, 177
Go and catch a falling star, 38
Go, lovely rose, 162
Græcinus (well I wot) thou told'st me once, 69

Had we but world enough, and time, 185

Have you seen but a bright lily grow, 16

Helen, thy beauty is to me, 168

Her eyes the glow-worm lend thee, 21

Her feet beneath her petticoat, 18

Her hair the net of golden wire, 160

Here ends this cycle of my poems for you, 144

His heart, to me, was a place of palaces and pinnacles and shining towers, 101

Horses of summer, 149

How can I hinder or restrain my soul, 204

How do I love thee? Let me count the ways, 205

How fond, how fierce, your arms to me would cling, 30

How instant joy, how clang, 169

How like a winter hath my absence been, 182

How many times do I love thee, dear, 167

How prone we are to sin; how sweet were made, 45

How sweet I roamed from field to field, 77

I am a quiet gentleman, 57

I arise from dreams of thee, 166

I asked my fair, one happy day, 52

I asked the heaven of stars, 57

I cannot live with you, 87

I care not for these ladies, 176

I cry your mercy—pity—love—aye, love, 81

I have been here before, 207

I have no life but this, 86

I hear some say, "This man is not in love!", 202

I knew a woman, lovely in her bones, 197

I know where I'm going, 189

I must not think of thee; and tired yet strong, 139

I prythee send me back my heart, 132

"I saw him kiss your cheek!"—" 'Tis true.", 54

"I shall be careful to say nothing at all, 59

I was so chill, and overworn, and sad, 142

I went to the garden of Love, 78

I will make you brooches and toys for your delight, 139

I will pluck from my tree a cherry-blossom wand, 25

I wish I could remember the first day, 8

I wonder do you feel today, 114

If thou must love me, let it be for naught, 205

Imperial Adam, naked in the dew, 126

In a nook, 196

In every solemn tree the wind, 101

In Love, if Love be Love, if Love be ours, 192

In our town, people live in rows, 125

In summertime on Bredon . . ., 99

In the merry month of May, 5

In the red April dawn, 8

"Is my team ploughing, 119

It is not, darling, in our power, 178

It is true love because, 63

It lies not in our power to love or hate, 3

It was a bowl of roses, 9

It was a lover and his lass, 4

It was not in the winter, 7

Jenny kissed me when we met, 23

Just imagine yourself seated on a shadowy terrace, 61

Kind are her answers, 75

Ladies, fly from Love's smooth tale, 36

Last June I saw your face three times, 95

Last night, ah, yesternight, betwixt her lips and mine, 97

Less than the dust beneath thy chariot wheel, 96

Let me not to the marriage of true minds, 180

Let's contend no more, love, 190

Lifting my eyes from Hesiod's great book, 174

Long have I borne much, mad thy faults me make, 68

Love laid his sleepless head, 195

Love's delight, 145

Loving you, flesh to flesh, I often thought, 199

Lying asleep between the strokes of night, 195

Man is for the woman made, 45

Mine by the right of the white election, 89

Miss J. Hunter Dunn, Miss J. Hunter Dunn, 62

"Mockery murders love," they say— and she, 173

More than most fair, full of the living fire, 151

Mother, I cannot mind my wheel, 84

Music, when soft voices die, 203

My Dear was a mason, 142

My girl is dark, but she is my desire, 174

My heart is like a singing bird, 137

My life close twice before its close, 89

My light thou art. Without thy glorious sight, 134

My love in her attire doth show her wit, 13

My sweetest Lesbia, let us live and love, 175

My true-love hath my heart, and I have his, 132

Nay, but you, who do not love her, 24

Never love unless you can, 35

Never seek to tell thy love, 23

"No! No! For my virginity, 49

No, No! Go from me. I have left her lately, 209

Not, Celia, that I juster am, 135

Now gentle sleep has closéd up those eyes, 40

Now sleeps the crimson petal, now the white, 192

Now that the chestnut candles burn, 106

O, for some sunny spell, 165

O, it was out by Donnycarney, 10

O, let the solid ground, 137

O Mistress mine, where are you roaming, 183

O my lover, blind me, 197

O my Luve's like a red, red rose, 165

O stay, sweet love; see here the place of sporting, 32

O sweetheart, hear you, 10

O wert thou in the cauld blast, 154

O Western wind, when wilt thou blow, 160

"O where hae ye been, Lord Randal, my son, 108

O whistle an' I'll come to ye, my lad, 188

Off all the souls that stand create, 88

Oh, see how thick the goldcup flowers, 56

Oh, when I was in love with you, 55

On his death-bed poor Lubin lies, 51

On yonder hill there stands a creature, 33

One day, it thundered and light-
ened, 53
Other beauties others move, 14
Out of your whole life give but a
moment, 193
Out upon it, I have loved, 43
Over the mountains, 187

Pack, clouds, away! and welcome,
day, 6
Phyllis! why should we delay, 184
Press close bare-bosom'd night—
press close magnetic nourishing
night, 169
Put out the fire and let the embers
die, 174

Remember me when I am gone
away, 90
"Rise up, rise up, now, Lord Doug-
las," she says, 109 ·

Seeing you smile, the furies fail to
stay angry, 130
Shall I compare thee to a summer's
day, 181
Shall I, wasting in despair, 40
She is as in a field a silken tent, 208
. . . She never told her love, 73
She shuts her eyes and keeps them
shut, 54
She walks in beauty, like the night,
166
Sigh no more, ladies, sigh no more,
36
Since fret and care are everywhere,
64
Since now, at last, we understand,
106
Since there's no help, come, let us
kiss and part, 73
Sing, ballad-singer, raise a hearty
tune, 94

So, we'll go no more a-roving, 81
somewhere i have never travelled,
gladly beyond, 26
Sorting out letters and piles of my
old, 105
Stay, O sweet, and do not rise, 76
Still to be neat, still to be drest, 15
Stop all the clocks, cut off the tele-
phone, 103
Sweet, can I sing you the song of
your kisses, 24
Sweet, let me go! sweet let me go, 44
Sweetest love, I do not go, 76
Swift boomerang, come get, 199

Take, O take those lips away, 74
Take this kiss upon the brow, 83
Tangled was I in Love's snare, 34
Tell me not, Sweet, I am unkind,
153
That which her slender waist con-
fined, 164
The brain forgets but the blood
will remember, 140
The fountains mingle with the river,
189
The grey sea and the long black
land, 115
The hope I dreamed of was a
dream, 90
The hunchéd camels of the night,
168
The lad came to the door at night,
121
The lark now leaves his watery nest,
3
The merchant, to secure his treas-
ure, 50
The moon shall be a darkness, 129
The moth's kiss, first, 191
The night has a thousand eyes, 209
The nightingale has a lyre of gold, 9
The praisers of women in their
proud and beautiful poems, 143
The rain set early in tonight, 116
The sea is calm tonight, 120

The seemingly lovely mourning dove is but a churl, 60
The soul selects her own society, 86
The time I've lost in wooing, 51
There is a lady sweet and kind, 160
There is no happier life, 135
They flee from me, that sometime did me seek, 71
This painful love dissect to the last shred, 211
Thou wast that all to me, love, 207
Tide be runnin' the great world over, 100

Under the willow-shades they were, 42

We stood by a pond that winter day, 94
What large, dark hands are those at the window, 122
What lips my lips have kissed, and where, and why, 102
When I am dead, my dearest, 91
When I was one-and-twenty, 55
When in disgrace with fortune and men's eyes, 181
When Love with unconfinéd wings, 133
When man shall find thy flower, thy glory, pass, 203
When my love swears that she is made of truth, 183
When our two souls stand up erect and strong, 206
When thou wilt swim in that live bath, 178

When we two parted, 82
When, with eyes closed in an autumnal dream, 194
When you are old and gray and full of sleep, 98
Whenas in silks my Julia goes, 21
White in the moon the long road lies, 98
Why, having won her, do I woo, 93
Why I tie about thy wrist, 19
Why shouldst thou swear I am forsworn, 42
Why so pale and wan, fond lover, 44
"Why those deep sighs?" I ask her, 54
Wild nights! Wild nights, 89
With all my will, but much against my heart, 92
With how sad steps, O Moon, thou climb'st the skies, 72
With wine and words of love and fervent vow, 174

Ye bubbling springs that gentle music makes, 31
Ye flowery banks o' bonie Doon, 79
You child, how can you dare complain, 58
You hypocrite, 141
You'll love me yet! And I can tarry, 7
Your hands lie open in the long fresh grass, 138
Your kisses, and the way you curl, 194
Your two great eyes will slay me suddenly, 70